AMERICAN WORDS AND WAYS

Especially for German Americans

American
WORDS AND WAYS

Especially for German Americans

BY JOHN WHYTE

1943

THE VIKING PRESS · NEW YORK

COPYRIGHT 1943 BY JOHN WHYTE

PRINTED IN U. S. A. BY VAIL-BALLOU PRESS

FIRST PUBLISHED BY THE VIKING PRESS IN JUNE 1943

PUBLISHED ON THE SAME DAY IN THE DOMINION OF CANADA
BY THE MACMILLAN COMPANY OF CANADA LIMITED

Preface

Among the foreign strains in America, the Germans rank high in their ability to adapt themselves to a new language and new customs and conventions. In this they are very fortunate, for the spiritual and material satisfactions which foreigners derive in their new homeland depend in no small degree on the ability to adjust to new surroundings and conditions. And it is equally true that the contributions which Germans can make to American civilization and culture stand in relationship to their ability and willingness to make adjustments. May this book serve this twofold purpose—the enhancement of personal satisfactions for Germans in America and the enrichment of American life by their contributions.

This book is not intended to replace the elementary English grammars which educated Germans have studied in Germany or in America. Though it contains a brief grammar review and word lists, it is not a systematic grammar. Moreover it differs from most grammars in one important aspect, for it lays particular stress on colloquial and informal English. Elementary grammars are usually designed for the purpose of providing the student with a reading knowledge of the literary language, and by their very nature pay little attention to informal, colloquial speech. The inevitable result of studying such grammars is a stilted, unnatural language, which by its formal literary correctness brands the user of it as a foreigner. "Dieser Mensch redet wie ein Buch—ist ein krankes Lob."

It is not easy to make distinctions in a language between formal, literary, and informal, colloquial usage. The line between the two is particularly difficult to draw in English, for informal English continually encroaches on formal English, and good colloquial English often serves as literary English. This book with its stress on the living English language in America ought to be a much

v

needed supplement to elementary English grammars, and a corrective for those who have taken their first steps in English with the aid of such grammars. To illustrate: Deutschbein's excellent *Grammatik der englischen Sprache* devotes only two lines to the important subject of contractions, mentioning only the contraction of *not* in such words as *can't, won't, couldn't*. Since these contractions, as well as a host of others, are continually used, not only in the "Umgangsprache," but in all but the most formal speech and writing, the follower of Deutschbein cannot avoid speaking very bookishly.

Since Deutschbein and other English grammars taught in Germany devote little or no space to English as spoken in America, I have included a chapter on the differences between British and American English in the belief that information on this interesting subject will be welcomed by those who began their study of English in German schools.

I have gone into far greater detail than does the usual grammar on some of the important differences between American English and German, differences in speech articulation, speech melody, the use of tenses, word order, punctuation, and syllabication. I could not within the space at my command make these analyses and observations exhaustive, needing to confine myself to outstanding differences.

I make no pretense, either, of exhaustiveness in listing the common errors in English to which Germans are addicted, nor have I been able to list these errors in the order of their frequency. But most of the common errors are, I believe, recorded, and the corrections I have supplied for them ought to be helpful not only to recent immigrants but to all who in their English are in any way influenced by their Muttersprache.

The differences between German and American customs, conventions, and temperaments were naturally the most difficult to formulate. Generalizations on such matters are never easy to make and they are always vulnerable to attack.

The reasons for this are obvious. Germans and Americans differ widely among themselves. Moreover, there are differences in both Germans and Americans that are due to differences in geographical, political, religious, cultural, class, and occupational backgrounds, to mention only a few. It is obviously impossible to take all these differences into account. I cannot in my comparisons and differentiations make allowances for the peculiarities of the Silesian, the Westphalian, the Rheinlander, the Bavarian, the Prussian, the Austrian, any more than I can for the Vermonter, the Indianan, the Southerner, and the Far Westerner. I have had to try to think in terms of the typical German and the typical American who in point of fact do not exist. My typical American is a cultured, educated American who belongs to no particular locality. My typical German is a cultured, educated German adult and it is to him that this book is addressed. Occasionally I have differentiated between the North and South German and between Americans of different professional and occupational groups. But I plead guilty to making broad generalizations. Germans who find some of these generalizations inapplicable to themselves will ignore them and the conclusions drawn from them.

When I point out differences in customs, conventions, and temperament, I do not mean ever to suggest a "Werturteil." I am merely interested in the fact of such differences and not in their moral or ethical implications. It is a question of "andere Länder, andere Sitten," and for the Germans in America, "When in America, do as the Americans do"—to paraphrase the Roman injunction. Wherever these differences are purely matters of external form, this injunction should not be difficult for a German to follow, for doing so involves no psychological strain. Adjusting the German temperament is, of course, another matter. For most Germans this adjustment will be an unconscious one that will, with children and adolescents, be fairly rapid and complete, but that can rarely be anything but gradual and slow with adults, and possibly never complete. But for German adults in America, a conscious, informed effort at adjustment based on a knowledge of differences in language and national temperament will speed up the process, at the same time that it will contribute to a deeper understanding of both America and Germany. And for those who make it in the spirit of high adventure, it may well become a fascinating and enriching human experience.

NOTE: For obvious reasons my book deals with pre-Hitler Germans and pre-Hitler Germany, and will presumably be read largely by Germans who came to America before Hitler's advent to power, or because of it.

Acknowledgments

In making acknowledgment of my indebtedness to the books and persons that have been helpful to me in the preparation of this book, I shall list first, the books that I have consulted and drawn on in the first part, which deals with speaking and writing American English, and second, my colleagues and friends who have aided me in the second and third parts, which deal with social forms and customs, and differences in national characteristics and temperaments.

With my constant emphasis on cultivated colloquial American English, I found little that I could use to advantage in the average handbooks of English, either those published in America or in Germany, for their point of view was either too literary, too traditionally grammatical, or too limited to serve my purposes. I needed, therefore, to go to the scholarly and inclusive grammars of Curme, Jespersen, and Fries, who have treated the English language, whether in America or Britain, as an ever-changing phenomenon that cannot be strait-jacketed by unchangeable, traditional grammar rules. And I found much in these sources for which I am grateful. My chapter on Shall and Will might not have been written without the studies of Professor Fries, though my treatment of this thorny problem is definitely my own. I am also indebted to him for his definition of colloquial American English. While I found little in Jespersen's four-volume grammar which I have quoted, I referred to it frequently while writing my book. My greatest debt, however, is to Curme's scholarly *Syntax,* on which I have drawn heavily for the chapters on Tenses, the Progressive, and the Abridgment of Clauses to Phrases. My chapter on Current Established Usage is an abbreviation and adaptation of the pioneer study of the late S. A. Leonard in this area. Deutschbein's *Grammatik der englischen Sprache* and Aronstein's *Englische Schulstilistik* sometimes served as points of departure and provided several illustrations. The chapters on American English and British English, and Standard Pronunciation in America owe something to Mencken's *The American Language* and O'Neill's *Foundations of Speech*. Fowler's *Dictionary of Modern English Usage* furnished material for my chapter on Word Order. Several examples of the wrong use of the Progressive were taken from an article by Professor Allen Porterfield on this subject.

In order to check my feeling for colloquial American English, I consulted many of my colleagues, particularly those in the field of English, both orally and by questionnaires. Professors Homer Watt of New York University, W. W. Watt of Lafayette College, William Ellery Leonard of Wisconsin, and Stanley Rypins of Brooklyn College not only responded freely to my questions, but by their interest in my project encouraged the hope that my book may prove interesting and valuable to teachers of English. I am greatly indebted to Virginia Harrington, Assistant to the Dean and Assistant Professor of History at Barnard College, for her excellent annotated bibliography on the American Way, and to Betty Drury, Executive Secretary of the Emergency Committee in Aid of Displaced Foreign Scholars, for several helpful suggestions.

The second and third parts of the book on social forms and differences in national characteristics were read in their entirety and criticized by three German American colleagues, Professor Hans Rosenberg of the History Department of Brooklyn College, Dr. Thea von Seuffert, formerly of the German Department of Russell Sage College, and Professor William R. Gaede of the German Department of Brooklyn College. Professor Rosenberg's historical approach was very helpful. Dr. Thea von Seuffert not only typed most of the manuscript, but offered many useful running comments on all the chapters, as the book took form. My departmental colleague, Professor Gaede, subjected every chapter to incisive, critical analysis, from which the book has greatly benefited. By placing their stamp of approval on the whole book, these friends must share with me, in a sense, whatever praise or censure it receives.

There are many other German Americans who have collaborated in the writing of this book, many of them quite unwittingly. If the book should prove helpful to them, my debt to them will be discharged. But I am conscious of a greater obligation to German Americans that cannot be so perfunctorily met. My book is the product of a life-long association with German Americans, to whose fine qualities of heart and head and loyal friendships I owe much of the happiness life has given me. I can only single out three, my former professors at Wisconsin, Professor A. R. Hohlfeld, Professor E. C. Roedder, now of the City College (New York), and Professor J. H. Ott of Northwestern College, to whose scholarly ideals, encouragement, and friendship I owe a lasting obligation.

And finally for encouragement and help in all the stages of work on the book, from the idea to the page proofs, I am deeply grateful to my wife, who contributed the largest share to the pleasant but sometimes arduous task.

JOHN WHYTE

Brooklyn College

Contents

CONTENTS

Social Forms and Social Customs in America

Differences in National Characteristics and Temperament

SPEAKING AND WRITING
COLLOQUIAL AMERICAN
ENGLISH

CHAPTER I

Standard Pronunciation in America

THE question, "What is the standard pronunciation in America?" is perplexing not only to foreigners, but to Americans as well. Whereas in German-speaking countries there is an accepted standard Bühnenaussprache, which is mandatory for the stage in all German-speaking countries and has some normalizing effect in unifying German speech, there is no such standard American speech, either for the American stage or for Americans generally. On the classic American stage some attempt is made to establish uniformity by adopting the speech of the classic British stage, or a close approximation of it. But consistency is rarely achieved and in the performances of Shakespeare in America one usually hears a wide variety of speech. For example, Lynn Fontanne speaks her lines in her native English tradition, while her husband, Alfred Lunt, though not speaking his native Wisconsin dialect, will hardly pass for an English actor. Similarly, Maurice Evans speaks his Shakespeare differently from Helen Hayes and the German-born Mady Christians in the same play, and the screen actor, Herbert Marshall, "doubles" as a cultured English or American gentleman without any change of pronunciation or speech tune. The average American audience appears wholly oblivious of conflicting speech patterns, when it hears these favorite actors.

There is then no easy answer to the question which every foreigner asks: How should I pronounce this word or read these lines? He was confronted with the same problem when he tried to learn British English, even though he may have been told that the best English is spoken by cultured Englishmen of the South of England. A philologically satisfactory answer to the problem of "the best English" is sometimes given by British and American phoneticians in their statement that THAT English pronunciation is best which reveals the fewest local speech characteristics and is at the same time most widely understood in all English-speaking countries—by the English, the Scots, the Irish, the Canadians, the Australians, the South Africans, and the Americans. But this theoretically perfect answer is not very satisfactory to the German learning English, though the point of view, as tending to eliminate local speech variants, may be helpful.

THE PRACTICAL APPROACH:

The German who desires to make a complete adjustment to his new country should obviously attempt to adjust his speech to American speech habits and patterns. How may he best do this in the absence of a single standard of American speech? The following considerations may provide him with the best possible solutions.

There are three large categories of speech in America.

1. EASTERN SPEECH (sometimes called New England speech) which is spoken by the majority of educated people in the New England States,[1] and eastern Canada.

2. SOUTHERN SPEECH, which is spoken by the majority of educated people south of the Potomac and Ohio rivers.

3. GENERAL AMERICAN SPEECH (sometimes called Middle Western speech) which is spoken by the majority of educated people west of the New England States and north of the Southern States, including central and western Canada.

Since by far the greatest number of Americans speak General American speech, this speech might well be imitated, though it

---

[1] The speech of educated people in New York City, though bearing a strong resemblance to Eastern speech, is different from that of New England, and is often classified separately. Roughly estimated, Eastern speech is spoken by about 15 millions, Southern speech by 30 millions, and General American speech by 90 millions.

would be important for Germans to avoid certain peculiarities of speech of the real, the GEOGRAPHICAL Middle West, such as the typical dorsal Middle Western *r,* the "flatness" and the nasality of much of this speech—which last ought to be easy, since most Germans are not addicted to nasality.

The New Englanders, as one of the oldest groups in America, like to think of their speech as the best American speech (somewhat as the Hanoverians think of their German), and, except when it is too much affected by a Yankee nasal twang, as in the case of Calvin Coolidge and those who speak like him, New England speech is accepted as cultured American speech and is therefore a good model to follow. Excessively "Hahvud" speech, which however is not spoken by such Harvard men as President Conant, is as much to be avoided as the peculiarly Oxford or Cambridge speech is avoided by the average cultured Englishman.

No speech in America so quickly reveals the origin of the speaker as does the speech of the Southerner with its characteristically slow tempo or pace and its excessive drawl.

ADJUSTING TO THE SPEECH OF YOUR COMMUNITY:

In the light of these considerations, it would seem that the best advice to follow would be: Make an attempt to adjust your speech to that of the community in which you live. In other words, if a German lives in New England, he should adjust himself to the cultured speech of his surroundings and not necessarily attempt to speak General American speech, simply because it is the speech of the majority of Americans. Similarly, if he lives in the states west from New England to California, Washington, and Oregon, he should try to imitate the cultured speech of his surroundings in these states, and not inflict a New England speech upon his neighbors, simply because someone has told him that "the speech of New England is a more cultured variety." But a German living in the South cannot follow this advice successfully, for the chances are wholly against his ever completely appropriating Southern speech. He is too far removed from the Southerner in his temperament and speech patterns ever to acquire Southern speech perfectly. All he can do, therefore, is to achieve some linguistic compromise, even at the expense of being taken for a "Yankee."

CHAPTER II

An Analysis
of Radio Speakers

THE radio offers English lessons to foreigners most inexpensively and most effectively. Think of the possibility, by a mere turn of a knob, of commanding hundreds of speakers a week to speak to you in your own home. The advantage of the radio over the newspapers and books is, of course, in the reproduction of the spoken word and hence the possibility of learning American pronunciation. The following brief paragraphs may prove helpful to the German in choosing which speakers he should imitate.

Serious efforts are now being made by all the large radio companies to improve the speech of their regular announcers. Though the results of these efforts are sometimes amusing, as when some of the announcers depart so far from their native speech as to sound affected, most of the announcers are now good models to follow.

COMMENTS ON PROMINENT RADIO SPEAKERS:

PRESIDENT ROOSEVELT: President Roosevelt's speech is accepted by most Americans as an excellent example of cultured American speech. Though a native of New York State, President Roosevelt has none of the so-called Middle Western characteristics of many inhabitants of this state. His speech is not nasal and it is carefully enunciated, though not affectedly so. In common with New Englanders and many others on the Eastern seaboard, he drops the final *r*. Though educated at Groton and Harvard, his speech is not noticeably Harvardian.

ELMER DAVIS, of Indiana, belongs to the general American group, but his speech is a typically Middle Western variety, which corresponds perfectly to his natural, direct, straightforward, and unemotional vocabulary and general manner of speech. Though his speech is Middle Western in its flatness and lack of modulation, it avoids the slovenly and overnasal quality of much Middle Western speech, is clear and distinct, and hence a good model for Germans residing in the Middle West to follow.

WENDELL WILLKIE (a fellow Indianan) also speaks a typically Middle Western variety of American speech, with, however, a great deal of the slovenly character of enunciation which is often heard in the Middle West. Examples of this are his continual substitution of *d's* for *t's* as in "budder," for "butter," "wader" for "water," and his dropping of the *t's* in "We want to win this war," which becomes "We wanna win this war." His *r* is the typical dorsal Middle Western *r,* which does strange things, e.g., making "Amairican" sound like "Amurican." It would take a great deal of effort for Germans to imitate this speech. For that reason alone, but also because of the examples given above, Mr. Willkie's speech should not be imitated by Germans.

EDWARD R. MURROW has a speech that is in the general American manner, but it is more carefully enunciated than the speech of the average American in this group, without sounding affected in any way. It has none of the flatness or nasality of much of American speech and achieves a certain distinction by a careful and apparently unstudied modulation. Germans will find it easier to imitate than the speech of Elmer Davis.

QUINCY HOWE's speech is his own peculiarly "Yankee" brand of New England speech, excessively nasal and with a strange pronunciation of the *ā* sound in day, which he pronounces as though it were the umlauted *ä*.

RAYMOND GRAM SWING's speech belongs in the general American group, though he has made concessions to Eastern pronunciation. His speech is clear, distinct, and cultivatedly cultured, and though possibly too carefully modulated, it is a very impressive kind of platform utterance.

CLIFTON FADIMAN (Interlocutor of the "Information Please" Group), a native New Yorker, has stripped his speech of New Yorkese, if he ever had it, and now speaks the cultured speech of the literary critic of the Eastern seaboard.

JOHN KIERAN's speech is of the New York City variety without, however, sounding particularly New Yorkese. Though his pronunciation of words is Eastern, his whole manner of speech is utterly American of the general American type.

OSCAR LEVANT talks (not speaks) the "roughneck" speech of the consciously "tough" city boy of New York City or of Pittsburgh, his native city. His speech belongs in the general American group. It has never made any concessions to the speech of his schoolteachers.

FRANKLIN P. ADAMS speaks with an admirable crispness for a native Chicagoan. He has made some concessions to the speech of the Eastern seaboard. But the concessions he made to one of his grade school teachers of English are outstanding. An English teacher once told him that the unaccented *or* in such words as lab*or*, act*or* and hum*or* must be pronounced to rhyme with bore or Ruddigore. His persistence in giving these unaccented syllables the *or* quality instead of their inevitable *er* quality, e.g., laber, acter, humer, makes this aspect of his otherwise excellent speech sound hopelessly "schoolmarm." *Humorous* and *numerous* and *humor* and *roomer* are exact rhymes, regardless of the spelling, for one rhymes by ear and not by eye in the unphonetically spelled English language.

DOROTHY THOMPSON's speech, once undoubtedly general American, is now the speech of a cultured speaker of the East, without, however, being the exact speech of either cultured New Yorkers or New Englanders. Whether her present speech was originally affected or not, it now has an authentic pattern of its own and would be an excellent model for German women to follow.

H. V. KALTENBORN's speech is characterized by a crispness and clearness of enunciation, which, however, by its very crispness and incisiveness, and occasionally also by its speech tune, reveals his Wisconsin German background. It is therefore obviously the kind of speech that Germans can imitate much more successfully than the more typically American speech of the Roosevelts, the Davises, the Murrows, the Willkies, and the Kierans.

CHAPTER III

American English and German Sounds

THE major general differences in enunciation and speech tune between American English and German may be summarized as follows.

1. The basis of enunciation is much farther back in the mouth in English than in German—except for the *ach, r,* and the glottal stop (Kehlkopfverschlusslaut) sounds.

2. English vowels and diphthongs are longer than corresponding German vowels and diphthongs.

3. English consonants are spoken with much less breath, are less abruptly cut off, and less explosively propelled or expelled than German consonants.

4. Initial accented vowels in English are less explosively expelled.

5. There is less physical effort in English speech than in German, less "Kraftaufwand," less energy.

6. Accented syllables and words in English carry less stress than accented syllables and words in German.

7. The weaker dynamic stress (paragraphs 5 and 6) lowers the average pitch of the voice in English and results in smaller intervals of tone between accented words or syllables and between accented and unaccented words or syllables.

8. The American speaks with less emotion than the German, giving to words, phrases, and sentences of a moderate or high degree of emotional content much less stress than the German.

9. The general impression that American English makes on

German ears is one of smoothness, evenness, and monotony as against the explosive, uneven quality of German.

10. English speech melody differs from German speech melody particularly in the absence of the regularly recurrent sharply rising inflection before pauses and commas, which is so characteristic of German speech.

INDIVIDUAL SOUNDS IN AMERICAN ENGLISH:

These major differences may be illustrated by an analysis of individual English sounds, particularly of those that cause Germans the most trouble.

1. The *p, t,* and *k* sounds in English have much less breath than in German, though they seem to be identical sounds. If you can hold a lighted match three inches away from your mouth and speak the words papa, tattoo, cocoa (*k* sound) without blowing out the light, you are probably speaking the sounds correctly. You will always (unless you are "sächsisch") blow out the match when speaking the German words Papa, tätig, Kakao. Reduce the breath on these sounds everywhere (*anlautend, inlautend,* and *auslautend*).

2. The *b, d,* and *g* sounds in English are, at the beginning of words, very much like the German *b, d,* and *g.* But at the end of words in German these sounds become *p, t,* and *k* (thus Tag is pronounced Tak,[1] hab' becomes hap and gab' becomes gap). Germans are therefore likely to carry over this speech habit into English and pronounce sob as sawp, god as gawt, and dog as dawk, which is very bad. The English words must retain the FINAL B, D, AND G SOUNDS. In addition, the vowel sounds in all these words must be lengthened, or diphthongized.

3. The English *l* sound is a much thicker, darker sound than the German *l* and is spoken farther away from the teeth and the tip of the tongue. Thus, the English name Willie sounds to Ger-

---

[1] In the Bühnenaussprache.

man ears very much like *Woolie* or *Wullie* and bears little resemblance to the crisp, precise *Willy* with its pure *i* vowel and
frontal *l*. While this *l* in Woolie is too thick, the German should
attempt to achieve a sound between his clean, precise *l* and the
thick, dark American *l*. (The British *l* is crisper and brighter
than the American.)

4. Though the German and English *s* sounds are considered
identical sounds for phonetic transcription, most Germans have
great difficulty in pronouncing the English *s* sounds without a
German accent, both the unvoiced *s* in "house" and "moss" and the
voiced *s* sound in "stairs" and "cares." The German in pronouncing the final unvoiced *s* sound in "house" and "moss" is likely to
speak it too breathfully, concentrating the breath at a narrow point
and also protracting the sibilant or hissing sound. In English, this
sound is spoken with less breath, and less concentrated breath, and
the sibilance or hissing ceases almost immediately, once the sound
is produced. Hence, shorten the *s* sound.

It is, however, the *voiced s* sound, particularly at the end of
words, that causes Germans the greater difficulty. One reason for
this is that Germans have only an *unvoiced s* at the end of words,
e.g., "Gas." They are thus likely to pronounce the final *s* in such
words as "stairs," "cares," "goes" with the pointed, protracted
hissing sound of the German *s* in "Gas," instead of giving it the
sound of *s* in "lösen." South Germans and Austrians, who use
only the unvoiced *s* in all positions in German, need particularly
to practice the voiced *s* sound in English, not only at the end of
words, but medially, e.g., in "houses." Germans, who in English
speak too sibilantly (as described above), give the effect of lisping
to American ears.

To SUMMARIZE: Distinguish carefully between the voiced and
unvoiced *s,* reduce the breath and also shorten the sound, and
lower the tongue, withdrawing it slightly from the teeth.

5. One of the difficulties which Germans have with the American *r* may be quickly removed by dropping the *r,* as many Ameri-

cans in New England, the Eastern seaboard generally, and the
South do, at the end of words and syllables, in fo-$_{uh}$ (four) and
fo-ty (forty), just as many Germans do in De$_a$ Bēlin$_a$ gab es mi$_a$
(der Berliner gab es mir). That still leaves the *r* at the beginning
of words and syllables in English. The first step is to omit the
trill in the German uvular or guttural *r*, the second, to eliminate
the uvular production entirely. To produce the English *r,* raise
the tongue and curl it back, and practice, practice, practice.

6. The *th* sound: One of the most difficult English sounds for
a German to learn is the *th,* which no longer exists in modern
German, though it was once a familiar sound in the court of
"Karl der Grosse." It is therefore not an un-Germanic sound and
can be learned with a little practice. The phonetic description of
it, as given in Ripman's *English Phonetics,* is as follows: When
the breath issues between the tips of the upper teeth and the tongue,
the resulting sound is the voiceless *th* (as in thin) or the voiced *th*
(as in this). The tongue may be between the teeth, and the sounds
are accordingly sometimes called interdental, but this is by no
means essential. Our English lisping sounds are usually produced
between the point of the tongue and the back of the upper front
teeth; part of the tongue fills up the small gap between the upper
and lower teeth, without advancing beyond their back surface.

For the foreigner who has to be taught this sound the simplest
injunction is: "Put your tongue between your teeth and blow."

ENGLISH AND GERMAN VOWEL SOUNDS:

The first step in learning to pronounce English vowels is a major
operation, the removal of the so-called glottal stop or glottal catch
(der Kehlkopfverschlusslaut) which precedes every *accented* initial vowel in German. It is the same sound that we hear when
we clear our throats, and let the breath come out violently and
in jerks. It sounds like a cough, a little nervous cough. It is this
little cough or catch in the throat which, preceding every accented
German vowel, gives to German speech its peculiarly explosive,

jerky effect, and it must be eliminated from English FIRST OF ALL and AT ALL COSTS. But how eliminate it?

The following exercise may "do the trick." Take for example two lines from the lovely Heine lyric, "Du bist wie eine Blume":

> "Mir ist, als ob ich die Hände
> Aufs Haupt dir legen sollt"

Read them first with a strong accent on every accented initial vowel. That will be speaking 'ist, 'ob, and 'aufs with a glottal stop. Then try to eliminate the stop by making a very slight liaison between mir and ist (mirist) and between als and ob (alsob). Then try to start the *au* sound in 'aufs in the cavity of your head and not in your throat, and you will see and hear what is meant. Now try singing these lines in the Schumann setting, both with the explosive glottal stop sounds with 'ist, 'ob, and 'aufs, and then with the smooth legato enunciation that would be given to these accented vowels by a Liedersinger, who has the sensation of dropping them down from the top of his head cavity, or at least of forming them all in his mouth, and not first in his throat.

IMPURE ENGLISH VOWELS VERSUS PURE GERMAN VOWELS:

German vowels are relatively pure; even long, protracted (gedehnte) German vowels retain at the end of the sound the essential character of the vowel at its beginning. That is not true in English. As compared with German vowels, English vowels are impure. The long ones change their character greatly, and even the short ones are impure. A few examples will illustrate this point: The German long vowel sound in such words as "Reh" and "Fehl" retain pretty much their pure character, but the so-called same sounds in English in "day" and "fail" trail off into other sounds. Thus day becomes day^{ee} and fail becomes fay-ul. And so it goes with one vowel after another. The *o* in no is not like the German *o* in so, but it is no^u. The *oi* sound in boy is not the *oi* sound in the German Heu, but boy[ee]. Dog becomes daw-ug, God becomes Gaw-ud, girl becomes gir-ul, boil becomes boi-ul.

Even short vowels in English change their character as they are lengthened. Him becomes hi-im with a difference in the two *i's*. Hill becomes hi-ull, saw becomes saw-uh, etc.

Learn therefore to drawl (draw-ul) your English vowels. Let them go up or down the musical scale, as the case may be; don't cut them off short; use glissandos and portamentos on them.

And one point more. SPEAK ALL YOUR ENGLISH VOWELS FARTHER FROM YOUR TEETH AND THE TIP OF YOUR TONGUE THAN YOU SPEAK THE CORRESPONDING GERMAN VOWELS.

FINAL COUNSEL:

When you have learned most of the individual English sounds, go back to the summary at the beginning of this chapter (page 11) and read some English sentences in a leisurely, unemphatic, un-emotional manner, drawling your vowels, reducing the breath on your consonants, and the result is likely to be something close to American English. It will all sound strange to you at first, this conscious affectation of unemotional, untense American speech and of the American temperament, but you can't speak American English with the German intensity of enunciation and a German temperament. So act a part until it becomes second nature to you.

PRACTICE WORDS AND SENTENCES:

god—gaw-ud

dog—daw-ug

day—day-[ee]

say—say-[ee]

hail—hai-ul (hay-ul)

so—so-[u]

no—no-[u]

girl—gir-ul

boy—boy-ee

boil—boi-ul

fall—fa-ul

doll—da-ul

my—my-[ee] (mai-[1])

mine—mi-[in] (mai-[in])

file—fi-ul (fai-[ul])

Say, it's a fine day today
Say[ee], it's a fai-[in] day[ee] today[ee].

I feel well
I fee-ul we-ul

She's so nice
She's so[u] ni-[is] (nai-[is])

NOTE: I have not used the standard phonetic transcriptions, but English or German approximations of them.

A COMPARISON OF TYPICAL ENGLISH AND GERMAN SPEECH MELODIES:

In his Anhang to *Übungen im englischen Tonfall,* Klinghardt uses so-called Punktbilder for recording virtually identical English and German sentences. (Klinghardt follows the English intonation of England, but in the sentence cited, the American intonation is identical with the English. The comma symbol denotes a downward glide, the inverted comma symbol an upward glide. The larger dots denote stresses. See page 18.)

A comparison of the two Punktbilder shows the following characteristics of English and German speech melody. (a) In English we begin each of the first three phrases with a relatively high pitch on the first accented syllable or word, then the pitch tends to drop to the end of the phrase so that even an upward glide at the end does not bring the pitch so high as it was on the accented syllable at the beginning. (b) In German we begin each of the first three phrases with a relatively high pitch on the first accented syllable, then lower the pitch, but RAISE IT at the end of the phrase usually far ABOVE THE PITCH OF THE ACCENTED SYLLABLE AT THE BEGINNING OF THE PHRASE. (c) The last syllables in German at the END OF THE SENTENCE are far below the average pitch, much farther than the last syllables in English. (d) The difference in pitch between the high tones and low tones is much greater in German than in English. (It is of course possible to read the German sentence without raising the pitch as often or as high as Klinghardt does, but his reading is nevertheless typically German. It is also possible to read the English sentence differently from Klinghardt's reading. Most of my students in my classes in Phonetics, e.g., regularly read the second phrase—was once away in the country—as though there were a period after country. They simply let their voices fall, thus avoiding even the suspicion of an upward glide.)

a well-known dramatist

was once away in the country

when he unexpectedly received

an anxious letter from his wife

ein bekannter Dramatiker

war einmal aufs Land gereist

als er plötzlich von seiner Frau

einen besorgten Brief erhielt

Another example may serve further to illustrate this difference between the English and German speech tunes.

"Wir sind in das Hotel gegangen, da kommt die Kapelle rein, da haben wir getanzt, das hat uns gut gefallen" has the following melody:

```
                                                              rein
                    gang-en                              le
              ge-                                    pe
         tel
    sind in                            kommt
         das                                die
Wir             Ho-               da           Ka
```
_____

```
         tanzt
                              gut
                  hat
    haben wir        das      uns
                                  ge-
da          ge-                  fal-
                                    len
```

The English of this sentence would be spoken as follows:

```
              tel
    went to  ho-      band
         the                in
                         came
We              the
```
_____

```
      danced   had   good
                a
then we     and         time
```

Though it is possible to read both of these sentences slightly differently, the recordings given above are typical. A comparison of the two tunes will show that the American does not regularly raise his pitch before EACH pause, or if, or when he does, it does not reach the same high pitch. There is, in most conversational German, a RECURRING rise before EACH comma, with the pitch being highest before the commas and being maintained at virtually the same high level. Germans should therefore avoid this recurring high pitch before commas, and cultivate the high pitch on the FIRST accented word of the English sentence.

CHAPTER IV

Definition of Colloquial
American English

IN order that there may be no misunderstanding of terms, the following chapters are prefaced by a note on the word *colloquial* which Professor Charles Carpenter Fries wrote for his discussion of colloquialisms in his *American English Grammar*.[1]

"The word *colloquial* as applied to English words and structures is frequently misunderstood, even by teachers of English. Some confuse it with *localism,* and think of the words and constructions marked 'colloquial' as peculiarities of speaking which are characteristic of a particular locality. Others feel that some stigma attaches to the label 'colloquial' and would strive to avoid as *incorrect* (or as of a *low level*) all words and phrases so marked. The word *colloquial,* however, as used to label words and phrases in a dictionary like Webster's *New International Dictionary* has no such meaning. It is used to mark those words and constructions whose range of use is primarily that of the polite conversation of

---

[1] This book, which bears the sub-title *The Grammatical Structure of Present-Day American English with Especial Reference to Social Differences or Class Dialects,* was published by the National Council of Teachers of English, financed by it and supported also by the Modern Language Association and the Linguistic Society of America.

Fries's book and *Facts About Current English Usage* (also published by the National Council of Teachers of English in 1932—a development of an earlier study by S. A. Leonard) serve as a point of departure for some of my paragraphs on colloquial usage, and provide in addition many examples. The application of this material for the purposes of this book and the inclusion of a great amount of other material is the result of my own observations and investigations and of my own feeling for colloquial English. However, I have continually checked my feeling for current colloquial American English with that of a large number of educated native Americans, and my quoted examples are all of recent date.

Both books may be procured from D. Appleton-Century Company.

cultivated people, of their familiar letters and informal speeches, as distinct from those words and constructions which are common also in formal writing. As a matter of fact, even the language of our better magazines and of public addresses has, during the last generation, moved away from the formal toward the informal."

CHAPTER V

The Use of Contractions

IN his *Grammatik der englischen Sprache,* Deutschbein has the following brief note on contractions: "In der Umgangssprache verschmilzt die 'Negation' *not* gewöhnlich mit dem Hilfsverb. Es entstehen dann folgende Formen: I can't, I couldn't, I shan't, I shouldn't, I won't, I wouldn't." This brief reference to contractions and the implication in it that contractions are used only with the negation *not,* gives an utterly false picture of the use of contractions in English, both in British and American English. Contractions in English are so commonly used that their absence results in stilted, unnatural language. The long list of contractions given below are not only generally used in cultivated colloquial speech; they may also be used in informal letters and in all but the most formal public speeches and addresses. They constitute, of course, acceptable literary English in plays, short stories, and novels, wherever the author tries to reproduce spoken dialogue. Germans who desire to remove the last trace of foreignism from their speech should cultivate their use studiously.

Examples:

I'm here, he's here, she's here, it's here, we're here, you're here, they're here, for I am here, he is here, etc.

I'll be there, he'll be there, etc., for I will be there, he will be there, etc.

I shan't do it, he shan't do it, etc., for I shall not do it, he shall not do it, etc.

I won't do it, he won't do it, etc., for I will not do it, he will not do it; it won't do, for it will not do; I'll not do it, for I will not do it.

I don't care, we don't care, they don't care, etc., for I do not care, we do not care, etc. Note however that the contraction for the third person singular is he doesn't care, she doesn't care, and not he don't care, she don't care—formations by analogy which are not yet acceptable.

I wasn't coming, he wasn't coming, etc., for I was not coming, etc.

I'd rather stay, he'd rather stay, etc., for I would rather stay, I had rather stay, etc.

I'd like to, he'd like to, we'd like to, etc., for I would like to, he would like to, we would like to.

Contractions are particularly to be recommended in negative questions with the negative *not*. Thus, Isn't she coming? Won't she come? Hasn't she come? Couldn't she come? Didn't she come? The unabbreviated forms, Is she not coming? Will she not come? Has she not come? Can she not come? Would she not come? Could she not come? Did she not come? etc., all sound hopelessly unnatural in conversation, and the contracted forms are greatly to be preferred.

Contractions are very common in the perfect and past perfect tenses: I've been there, you've been there, he's been there, and I'd been there, they'd been there, etc., for I had been there, they had been there, etc.

Smith's here, Karl's come, for Smith is here, Karl has come, are usually used instead of the uncontracted forms. Similarly, Here's to you, Here's how, That's fine, Let's go.

NOTE 1. There is no satisfactory contraction for "Am I not?" Ain't I? and Aren't I? are still not acceptable and should be avoided. Americans with a feeling for cultivated colloquial English balk at the stilted quality of Am I not? and substitute some other expression for it. Thus instead of saying, "Am I not looking well?" they will use the paraphrase, "Don't you think I'm looking well?"

NOTE 2. The contractions mayn't and shan't are on the whole less frequently used in America for two reasons: (1) can and will are colloquially usually substituted for may and shall; (2) the uncontracted negation *not* is frequently demanded in these combinations. Thus, Father, may I stay up until eleven tonight? Father says, No, you may nót, with a very strong accent on *not*.

If the negation needs to be stressed very much, the uncontracted forms may be used, but there is little difference in meaning between I did nót come with a strong accent on *not,* and I *dídn't* come with an equally strong accent on the first syllable of *dídn't*. However, in refuting charges and statements the unabbreviated forms are frequently used. Thus, You said you did. Answer, I did nót.

In Formal Literary English:

While contractions are virtually mandatory for informal English, many of them, particularly don't, won't, and can't,[1] but also many others, have been used and are frequently used in formal literary English. The following examples taken from a recent issue of *The New Republic* will serve to illustrate their use: [2]

1. It is not surprising that the Russians are beginning to wonder whether Chamberlainism *hasn't* come back after all, whether Churchill *isn't* carrying the umbrella, whether the United Nations strategy *doesn't* mean that the Americans and the British hope . . . to rule an Anglo-Saxon world during what Mr. Luce calls the American Century. . . . Why *hasn't* Mr. Churchill bothered to clean out his Cabinet? He *hasn't* done it, because he *doesn't* see its importance.

2. We *don't* doubt that Kaiser has his faults. We *don't* doubt, either, that unless we can get rid of the sort of men who have worked so hard to prevent using him, we stand a chance of losing the war.

3. We *don't* know exactly what kind of country is needed to win a total war nowadays; but we know the kind of country that is likely to lose one. It is a country where . . . millions of radio listeners *won't* listen to radio messages from the gov-

---

[1] Cannot, written as one word, is obviously an intermediate step between the very formal can not, and the informal can't.

[2] Author's italics.

ernment unless they are towed in the wake of a favorite comedian.

The editors of this journal (which enjoys the reputation of being well written) would presumably justify these contractions as being called for in hard-hitting editorials—their very informality makes for forcefulness and directness.

There are fewer instances of contractions to be found in the English of book review sections, but even here they may sometimes be found. The following sentence is taken from a book review that appeared in the same issue of *The New Republic* which printed the above passages:

> To read Joyce was once the mark of high awareness; but now he has been put, along with Sanskrit, on the shelf of the things one *doesn't* get around to because they take too much effort.

In his review of Herbert Agar's *A Time for Greatness* (the leading review in the *New York Times Book Review* of October 4, 1942) Rex Stout uses contractions in order to make his words forceful, direct, and personal. Thus,

> That plane trip didn't get Agar into the war. He's been in it for a long time now. . . . It isn't just another anti-Nazi tract. . . . I'd like to see this one read by every WRONG-thinking American.

To Recapitulate:

Cultivate the use of contractions for all informal speaking and writing, and don't hesitate to use them occasionally in formal English.

CHAPTER VI

Eliminating
the Relative Pronoun
in Restrictive Clauses

E LIMINATING the relative pronoun in the objective case in restrictive clauses is a very common practice in English. It is almost always done in conversation and has sufficient literary authority behind it to establish it as acceptable in formal writing. Though Macaulay and Samuel Johnson opposed it, the great majority of writers in England and America may be cited as approving it. Jespersen, in his 4-volume *Modern English Grammar,* gives numerous illustrations of it, some of which (with others) will be given here.

EXAMPLES:

He knows the man you met yesterday (whom you met).
He's the man we spoke to (whom we spoke to).
It's an apple he wants, not a pear (that he wants).
What is this I hear about you? (that I hear about you).
All he could do was to tell his mother (all that he could do).
He did not notice the constraint the newcomer produced (which the newcomer produced).

In all the above examples, the addition of the relative pronoun would, in conversation, make for stilted speech, and should therefore be avoided. Its use in literary English is, except for purists, a matter of no great importance, and may be left to the discretion of the writer, who may drop the relative pronoun or use it, though he may want to retain it in very elevated prose.

Such ellipses are also common in prepositional phrases. Take the following sentence: "That is the way in which I played the shot," is, both in conversation and even in formal English, reduced either to "That is the way that I played the shot," or to "That's the way I played the shot," with the last variant being the most frequently used. Similarly, "They came the day we left," is more frequent than "They came the day that we left," and much to be preferred to the bookish "They came the day on which we left." (Note also the ellipsis "the day," for "on the day.") There may be little to choose between "That's the reason why I did it," and "That's the reason that I did it," and "That's the reason I did it," but the trend in English is all toward "That's the reason I did it."

OTHER EXAMPLES OF THIS USAGE ARE:

In prepositional phrases—

The pencil I wrote with was sharp.
The train I rode on was crowded.
The town I go to is right on a lake.
The city I come from is Watertown.
The day he arrived, it rained hard.
The year I left, we had a good harvest.
The reason I did it was this:

In subordinate clauses—

He's not the man he thinks he is.
He felt it in the merry sound of the regimental music he heard from the left side of the field, and felt and realized it especially from the list of soldiers the trench officer had read out when he came that morning. (From Tolstoy's *War and Peace,* translated by Louise and Aylmer Maude.)

These abbreviated constructions are not a new phenomenon in English. They have the sanction of hundreds of years behind them, and are, in the words of Curme, "good natural English expressions" in both literary and colloquial English. They should therefore be cultivated not only for their own sake, but also because they will often remove the frequent query of Germans, "Shall I use *that* or *which* in this subordinate clause?"

CHAPTER VII

Omitting the Conjunction
That in Indirect Discourse
(Indirekte Rede)

A FAVORITE contraction in English is the omission of the conjunction *that* in clauses of indirect discourse. Since the Germans also frequently omit "dass" both in speech and writing in indirect discourse (cf. "Er sagte, er habe ihn nicht gesehen") this common usage ought to be easy to appropriate, were it not for a natural tendency on the part of foreigners to speak and write more formally in their acquired language than they do in their own.

The omission of *that* is virtually mandatory in conversational English. For example, "He said he didn't think he'd do it," is much more commonly used than the wooden, lengthy, "He said that he did not think that he would do it." Similarly, "He said he was there." "He thought he spoke perfect English."

It is difficult to set up rules for the omission or the use of *that* in formal written or spoken English. There can, however, be no doubt whatever that its omission is well established by usage, except with pedants and purists. The following examples taken from one issue of *The New Republic* are proof of its current good usage.

1. The OWI does not believe American people will listen to Government officials unless they are tricked into doing so, by having already tuned in to their favorite program [*that* omitted].

2. Those who hold this view believe we have been terribly

hampered by not having a real global strategy [*that* omitted].

3. I think I can say without prejudice [*that* omitted].

On the other hand it is not, of course, wrong or unidiomatic to use *that* in formal writing and in formal speeches, and its use there, by slowing up the pace of expression, may well make for greater impressiveness. In the solemn, elevated war speeches of both Roosevelt and Churchill, *that* is usually not omitted. But its use or non-use may be determined by other considerations as well. For example, in the spoken sentence, "Columbus said the earth is round," "the earth is round" may be construed as either direct discourse or indirect discourse. If the speaker wants to avoid this ambiguity, he will say, "Columbus said *that* the earth is round." Subtle stylistic or rhythmic reasons may also be determining factors in deciding for or against *that*. The little problem, if problem it is, is not brought nearer a solution by finding *that* used and omitted in the same written sentence, e.g., "He said he believed that a united command was necessary." The author of this sentence, if asked to justify both his use and his omission of *that*, might give three answers:

1. I did not want to have two *thats* in close proximity.

2. I wanted my *that* in the second clause for greater emphasis of that clause.

3. I just don't know why I did it.

Similar and Other Omissions of THAT in THAT Clauses:

Closely related to the examples above are two others taken from the same issue of *The New Republic*.

1. It seems to me it is evident that we do not have the unity we must have in order to win [*that* omitted and *that* used in the same sentence].

2. Some of us hate President Roosevelt because we believe he has made such serious mistakes he should be removed from

office. . . . Some of us, on the other hand, have an admiration for him beyond the power of expression to explain."

In the first sentence *that* is omitted after "we believe," and also after "such serious mistakes." This second omission of *that* instead of "such serious mistakes that" is probably rather infrequent in writing.

TO RECAPITULATE:

1. Omit *that* in informal speech.

2. Cultivate the omission of *that* in most of your informal and even your formal writing, except in very formal, elevated writing, or when its use is necessary for clarity, or for style and rhythm.

CHAPTER VIII

The Use of Present Tense Forms

THE function of the present tense is described identically for both English and German, and yet there are enough different uses of present tense forms in the two languages to require some attention. There is, of course, no difference in meaning between "There he is" and "There he comes," and "Da ist er" and "Da kommt er." There is, however, a very important difference in the use of the present tense forms in English and German to express futurity.

In German one may use and does very commonly use present tense forms for future action or future meaning. Thus, "Morgen gehe ich in die Stadt und kaufe mir einen Anzug" is quite as acceptable, and in conversation certainly more frequent than "Morgen werde ich in die Stadt gehen und (werde) mir einen Anzug kaufen." If this sentence stands alone, and not in answer to a question (direct or implied), it must not be translated into English by "Tomorrow I go to the city and I buy a suit." Similarly impossible are such translations as, "I think I give up the idea for this summer," "I think I telephone him about it," "I go to see him when I come to New York," "I think I invite him to my next party." SUCH TRANSLATIONS CONSTITUTE ONE OF THE MOST COMMON ERRORS OF GERMANS WHEN SPEAKING OR WRITING ENGLISH.

The correct sentences are: "Tomorrow I'm going (I'll go) to the city, and I'll buy a suit." "I think I'll give up the idea for this summer." "I think I'll telephone him about it." "I'll go (I'm going) to see him when I get to New York." "I think I'll invite him to my next party."

The Use of Present Tense Forms for Future Meaning:

Under certain definite conditions one may, however, use the present tense forms in English in the future meaning, namely, in answer to questions of time (either direct or implied). The question in such combinations may also be in the present tense. Thus, if the questions are, "When are you leaving for Chicago?" or "When do you leave for Chicago?" or "When will you leave for Chicago?" the answer is usually, "I leave tomorrow on the five-forty." Similarly the questions, "When does the train start?" "When does the contract expire?" "When do you begin work?" "When is your party?" are all usually answered, "The train starts in half an hour." "The contract expires in thirty days." "I begin work on the fifteenth." "My party is day after tomorrow." (There is nothing wrong with the future tense forms, such as "The train will start in half an hour," and "The contract will expire in thirty days," but they are less idiomatic than the sentences in their present tense forms.)

The Use of the Present Tense in Subordinate Clauses with Future Meaning:

Germans, who are cautioned against the use of the present tense forms for the future meaning, often cultivate the use of a future tense where Americans and Englishmen would use the present tense. Thus they are likely to say, "I shall discuss the matter with you when I shall see you," or "when I shall go into town." The future tense forms in these subordinate clauses, "when I shall see you" and "when I shall come into town," are wholly unidiomatic and must be avoided. The correct expression is, "I shall discuss the matter with you when I see you, or when I go into town."

NOTE. The progressive form in the present and other tenses will be treated in a separate chapter, particularly its use in the present tense for future meaning.

CHAPTER IX

The Future Tense
Shall *and* Will ; Going

A DISCUSSION of the future tense involves explaining the use of the auxiliaries *shall* and *will* and hence entering upon one of the most controversial matters in all English grammar. For generations the writers of English and American grammars and dictionaries have stated a few simple rules for their correct use, blithely unconscious of their actual use in both England and America. As a point of departure these "simple" rules will be restated here:

1. To express pure futurity use *shall* (should) in the first person, singular and plural, and *will* (would) in the second and third, singular and plural.

    Examples: I (we) shall go home.

    You (he, they) will go home.

2. To express determination (or making a promise) use *will* (*would*) in the first person, singular and plural, and *shall* (*should*) singular and plural, in the second and third.

    Examples: I *will* go in spite of what you say.

    They *shall* not pass.

    You *shall* give me the money.

3. In asking questions, use the form which you anticipate in the answers.

    Shall you go to the seashore this summer?

    (Answer: Yes, we shall.)

But these simple (?) rules, which every school child has learned, are constantly being violated in the language of educated Englishmen and Americans. And little wonder, for the rules in the form given above have never corresponded to language usage from Shakespeare down to the present day. Professor Charles Carpenter Fries of the University of Michigan, some fifteen years ago, recorded and examined twenty thousand instances of *shall* and *will*, occurring in (a) fifty British dramas produced during the last three hundred and fifty years, (b) eighteen British dramas from 1902 to 1918, and (c) eighteen American dramas from 1906 to 1918, and came to the statistically invulnerable but startling conclusion that in independent declarative sentences the *shall* forms have been almost eliminated from American usage in all three grammatical persons, though they are somewhat more frequent in England. In other words, *will* in *I will* and *we will* (and not *I shall, we shall*) are quite generally used in both America and England to express pure futurity (as well as determination).

Professor Fries also found that the tricky rule for questions was never, and is not now, in accord with usage either in England or in America, but that *shall* predominates overwhelmingly in the first person and *will* predominates overwhelmingly in the second and third person.

Applying these conclusions of Fries, a German will find himself (a) in the good company of a majority of English and American writers and speakers when he writes or says, I will, he will, we, you, they will, to express pure futurity, and (b) in the company of all but a few purists and a decreasing number of English teachers, when he asks, *Will* you go to the seashore this summer? or better, Are you going to the seashore this summer? instead of *Shall* you go to the seashore, for the *shall you* question is rarely used in America or England.

SHALL AND WILL AND THE ENGLISH PURIST:

It is still the current fashion of writers of English handbooks, who merely copy down the rules from previously printed grammars, to question these conclusions of Fries. Two well-known English lexicographers, Fowler and Bradley, find the use of *will*

(I will and we will) for pure futurity "a mark of Scottish, Irish, provincial or extra-British idiom," and refer to Fries and others, who have dared to point out the inadequacy of the rules, as "people who are not to the manner born." How they must blush when they find purely English writers from Shakespeare and Ben Jonson down to the present day violating these sacred rules. And how must that master of the English tongue, Winston Churchill, grate on their ears, when he speaks in "an extra-British idiom" and betrays the fact that he is "not to the manner born." The following examples from some of the solemn war speeches of Churchill are certainly not justified by the rigid rules of Fowler and the majority of English and American grammarians, even though a few subtler grammarians find it possible to explain them within more elaborate rules.

From Churchill's speech before the House of Commons, June 4, 1940, on the evacuation from Dunkirk:

> We shall not flag or fail. We shall go on to the end, we shall fight on the seas and oceans, we shall fight with growing confidence and growing strength in the air, we shall defend our Island, whatever the cost may be, we shall fight on the beaches, we shall fight on the landing grounds, we shall fight in the fields and in the streets, we shall fight in the hills; we shall never surrender. . . .

From his broadcast on February 9, 1941:

> We shall not fail or falter; we shall not weaken or tire. Neither the sudden shock of battle, nor the long-drawn trials of vigilance and exertion will wear us down. Give us the tools, and we will finish the job.

Surely this use of *shall* expresses determination and not pure futurity, and is not covered by the conventional rules. It may well be that, since *will* is so frequently used in the first person for pure futurity, it is losing its force for determination, and that *shall,* which is less and less used for pure futurity, may sound more emphatic, when stressed, than *will*. Moreover, *shall* lends itself phonetically to more emphatic utterance than the weaker consonant and vowel combination in *will*. But however that may be, there can be little doubt that Churchill's determination is at least as strongly expressed as that of the American soldier whose words, shortly before his death, are quoted in Ambassador Grew's *Report from Tokyo:*

> I will work; I will save; I will sacrifice; I will endure; I will fight cheerfully and do my utmost, as if the whole struggle depended on me alone.

The conclusion from this is that both *will* and *shall* express determination in the first person when emphasized, even though there is a longer tradition behind *will* for this purpose.

Churchill's use of *will* and *would*. From his talk before the House of Commons on the Munich Agreement, October 3, 1938:

> Having thus fortified myself by the example of others, I will proceed to emulate them. I will, therefore, begin by saying the most unpopular and most unwelcome thing. I will begin by saying what everybody would like to ignore or forget, but which must nevertheless be stated, namely, that we have sustained a total and unmitigated defeat, and that France has suffered even more than we have.

From his talk on the withdrawal from Norway:

> I would like to say a few things about the subject of the Norwegian campaign.

Fowler and his followers, whether English or American, can hardly justify these uses of *will* as falling under their simple rules.

Shall and Will are both Future and Modal Auxiliaries:

The confusion over *shall* and *will* derives largely from the stubborn philological fact that *shall* and *will* are not pure future auxiliaries, but also modals, and that their use as either future auxiliaries or modals must be clearly understood, or ambiguities will result. Fortunately for the German, this confusion can usually be cleared up by reference to the German *werden, wollen,* and *sollen.* For example, "Shall we see him tomorrow?" may mean either, "Werden wir ihn morgen sehen?" ("Sehen wir ihn morgen?") or "Sollen wir ihn morgen sehen?" On the other hand, the question "Shall we come tomorrow?" is surely normally not a future, equivalent to "Werden wir morgen kommen?" but rather to "Sollen wir morgen kommen?" How may this ambiguity be avoided, and future action be unambiguously expressed?

LEARN TO USE THE PERIPHRASTIC FORMS, We are going to see him, We are going to play, AND Are you going to see him? Are you going to play? TO EXPRESS FUTURE ACTION.

The American and Englishman can express future action by the use of the paraphrases with *going.* These paraphrases with *going* are usually the exact equivalent of the German *werden.* Moreover, they are cultivated, colloquial English and are used predominantly, except in the most formal literary English. THEY MUST, THEREFORE, BE LEARNED AND USED. The translation of "Werden Sie morgen spielen?" is "Are you going to play tomorrow?" and NOT the rarely used, puristic "Shall you play tomorrow?" or the "Will you play tomorrow?" which is a modal, virtually equivalent to "Wollen Sie morgen spielen?" or "Möchten Sie morgen spielen?"

FUTURE ACTION EXPRESSED BY THE PROGRESSIVE:

It is also possible to express future action in English by the use of the present progressive. Thus, "I am seeing him tomorrow," "I am playing tomorrow," and "Are you seeing him tomorrow?" "Are you playing tomorrow?" are the translations of "Ich werde ihn morgen sehen." ("Ich sehe ihn morgen.") and "Werden Sie ihn morgen sehen?" ("Sehen Sie ihn morgen?").

However, there is a subtle difference between the meaning of "I am going to see Jones tomorrow," and "I am seeing Jones tomorrow." Though these two sentences may often be used interchangeably, the sentence, "I am going to see Jones tomorrow," implies no knowledge on the part of Jones, who may know nothing about my future action or my intention. But, "I am seeing Jones tomorrow" usually suggests that I have an arrangement, an appointment with Jones. Similarly, "Are you going to play tomorrow?" is "Werden Sie morgen spielen?" whereas "Are you playing tomorrow?" usually implies a definite appointment, a date, a match, and is close to the German "Haben Sie sich für morgen verabredet?" Similarly, "Are you going to see the doctor tomorrow?" and "Are you seeing the doctor tomorrow?" with the second sentence implying an appointment.

The Conjugation of the Verb SEE with SHALL and WILL, and GOING:

A summary of the above paragraphs in the form of a conjugation with the German translations will further clarify these different uses.

Pure future action with going:

I am going to see him.	Ich werde ihn sehen.
He is going to see him.	Er wird ihn sehen.
We are going to see him.	Wir werden ihn sehen.
You, they are going to see him.	Sie, sie werden ihn sehen.

In a question:

Are you going to see him?	Werden Sie ihn sehen?

Future action with the present progressive:

I am seeing him (which often implies an appointment).	Ich werde ihn sehen (often—ich habe eine Verabredung).

In a question:

Are you seeing him? (implying an appointment).	Werden Sie ihn morgen sehen? (Haben Sie eine Abmachung, eine Verabredung mit ihm?)

Shall *and* will *as future and modal auxiliaries:*

WILL

I will see him.	Ich werde ihn sehen.
	Ich will ihn sehen.
He will see him.	Er wird ihn sehen.
	Er will ihn sehen.
We will see him.	Wir werden ihn sehen.
	Wir wollen ihn sehen.
You will see him.	⎰Sie (sie) werden ihn sehen.
They will see him.	⎱Sie (sie) wollen ihn sehen.

In a question:

Will I see him?	Werde ich ihn sehen?
	Will ich ihn sehen?
Will he see him?	Wird er ihn sehen?
	Will er ihn sehen?
Will we see him?	Werden wir ihn sehen?
	Wollen wir ihn sehen?
Will you see him?	Werden Sie ihn sehen?
	Wollen Sie ihn sehen?
Will they see him?	Werden sie ihn sehen?
	Wollen sie ihn sehen?

Whether the English *will* is the German *werden* or *wollen* often depends on the context. But the ambiguity may be avoided in two ways: (1) by using the paraphrase with *going* for the pure future *werden,* and (2) by using *want to* or *wish* for *wollen.* Thus, "When will the doctor see you again?" is either the German *wollen* or *werden.* When the meaning is the pure future, "When is the doctor going to see you again?" expresses the *werden* exactly, whereas "When does the doctor wish to (want to) see you again?" expresses the German, "Wann will der Arzt Sie wieder sehen?"

NOTE: Cultivate the contractions I'll, we'll, you'll, they'll, etc. in all but the most formal English. These are all contractions of *will*, and not of *shall*. If *will* is emphasized, it is not contracted. In negative emphasis, the contractions "I won't see him," "he won't see him" are often used instead of "I'll not see him," "he'll not see him."

SHALL

I shall see him.	Ich werde ihn sehen.
Thou shalt see him.	Du sollst ihn sehen.
He shall see him.	Er soll ihn sehen.
	(Er wird ihn sehen müssen.)
We shall see him.	Wir werden ihn sehen.
You shall see him.	⌠Sie (sie) sollen ihn sehen.
They shall see him.	⌡(Sie (sie) werden ihn sehen müssen.)

In a question:

Shall I see him?	Werde ich ihn sehen?
	Soll ich ihn sehen?
Shall he see him?	Soll er ihn sehen?
Shall we see him?	Werden wir ihn sehen?
	Sollen wir ihn sehen?
Shall you see him? (rarely used)	Werden Sie ihn sehen?
Shall they see him?	Sollen sie ihn sehen?

The ambiguity that attaches itself to the question, "Shall we meet you next week?" which is either "Werden wir Sie nächste Woche treffen?" or "Sollen wir Sie nächste Woche treffen?" may be partially avoided by using "Are we going to meet you next week?" for the pure future, and by reserving "Shall we meet you next week?" for "Sollen wir Sie nächste Woche treffen?"

THE FUTURE PROGRESSIVE:

For the meaning and force of the progressive forms, I shall be seeing him, I will be seeing him, consult the chapter on the progressive.

NOTE: Lest the reader think that I am trying to justify my own use of *shall* and *will*, let me assure him that as a result of years of subservience to the grammar rules, I in writing use *I shall* for pure futurity and not *I will*, and I shall presumably continue to do so. However, in informal speech I use *I'll* and *I'd*, the contractions of *I will* and *I would*, and not of *I shall* and *I should*. So far as I know, however, I have not used for years that strange question form, "Shall you go to Vermont this summer?"

CHAPTER X

The Subjunctive Mood
Should and Would

SHOULD and *would* present difficulties similar to those sur-
rounding *shall* and *will*. The German may, however, avoid
ambiguity and confusion in most cases by translating *sollte* by
should and *wollte* by *would*.

The sentence, "I should go if I could," may mean either, "Ich
würde gehen, wenn ich könnte," or, if *should* is slightly accented,
"Ich sollte gehen, wenn ich könnte." By reserving the use of *should*
for *sollte* and *would* for *würde,* the German may occasionally of-
fend a few purists, but he will be speaking and writing the language of the majority.

PRESENT ACTION IN THE SUBJUNCTIVE:

EXAMPLES:

I would go, if I could.
Ich würde gehen, wenn ich könnte.

He would go, if he could.
Er würde gehen, wenn er könnte.

PAST ACTION IN THE SUBJUNCTIVE:

EXAMPLES:

I would have gone, if I had been able to (had I been able to).
Ich wäre gegangen, wenn ich gekonnt hätte.

To express obligation, i.e., the German *sollen, should* is used in
all three persons.

I should know that.	Ich sollte das wissen.
He should know that.	Er sollte das wissen.
I should have known that.	Ich hätte das wissen sollen.

"I (he) would know that" corresponds to the German "Ich (er) würde das wissen."

In questions, *should* and *would* usually correspond to *sollte* and *würde,* though *would* may often be *wollte.*

EXAMPLES:

Should I (he) come?	Sollte ich (er) kommen?
Would he come?	Würde er kommen?
	Wollte er kommen?
Would he see me?	Würde er mich sehen?
	Wollte er mich sehen?

Just as *should* is compulsory for all three persons to express an obligation, *would* is compulsory to express customary or habitual action. Thus,

I (he) would take long walks every morning.
Jeden Morgen pflegte ich (er) lange Spaziergänge zu machen.

I (he) would go to the country in August.
Im August pflegte ich (er) aufs Land zu gehen (das war meine (seine) Gewohnheit).

OTHER EXAMPLES OF THE SUBJUNCTIVE:

If I were home, I would do it (should do it, for purists).
Wenn ich zuhause wäre, würde ich es tun.

"Were I home, I would do it," is less often used than "If I were home," but occurs frequently even in colloquial speech.

If I had been home, I would have done it.
Wenn ich zuhause gewesen wäre, hätte ich es getan.

"Had I been home, I would have done it," also occurs frequently in colloquial speech.

If he came, he might do it.
If he should come, he might do it.
If he had come, he might have done it.

Passive Voice:

If it were completed, it would be found unsatisfactory.
If it had been completed, it would have been found unsatisfactory.
Had it been completed, it would have been found unsatisfactory.

The subjunctives in the past and past perfect forms treated above cover the great majority of subjunctives in English. However, a few uses of the much less used present subjunctive need to be illustrated.

The Present Subjunctive:

The present subjunctive is often used after verbs (and adjectives) of advising, wishing, beseeching, warning, praying, demanding, deciding, etc.

Examples:

She asks that he consent to it.
He demands that it be done.
I insist that he follow.
The will provides that the estate be given to charity.
They decided that Karl play the part of the lover.

The present subjunctive is also used after clauses of purpose introduced by that, so that, in order that, for fear that, lest.

Examples:

I move that a committee be appointed.
Lest the reader think I am prejudiced, I shall state both sides of the case.
In order that there be no mistake, the words will be repeated.

If that be the case, there is nothing else to be done.
Be it ever so humble, there's no place like home.
It is sufficient that he come but once.
It is necessary that he come prepared for cold weather.

CHAPTER XI

The Present Perfect Tense

THE difficulties that Germans experience with the present perfect tense derive directly from their German speech patterns, which in many cases permit the substitution of the perfect tense for the past tense (or vice versa) with little or no change in meaning. Thus, in German, in narrating past events, one may say, "Wir sahen ihn gestern" or "Wir haben ihn gestern gesehen," with essentially the same meaning. The German perfect tense is therefore a tense of narration, which may be used for sentence after sentence, or alternated (for stylistic or other reasons that need not concern us here) with the past tense.

The English present perfect tense is definitely NOT a tense of narration and Germans must avoid using it for that purpose. While, in German, one may say (adding to the example given above), "Wir haben ihn gestern gesehen. Er hat sich uns angeschlossen und dann sind wir alle ins Kino gegangen," or "Wir sind in das Hotel gegangen, dann haben wir getanzt, und haben uns gut amusiert," these sentences must all be translated into the past tense in English, thus, "We saw him yesterday. He joined us, and we went to the movie," and "We went to the hotel, we danced, and we had a good time."

In learning the correct use of the perfect tense in English, it would be well for Germans to remember the word *present* in the term *present perfect,* for by definition (Curme, *Syntax*),[1] this tense in English represents an act as completed at the *present moment,* or felt as not wholly past, but at least in close relation with the *present.* Thus, "I have just finished my letter" (i.e., just a few

---

[1] Curme's *Syntax,* quoted here and elsewhere, is volume 3 of *Grammar of the English Language* by Curme and Kurath, published by D. C. Heath and Company.

moments ago, but not yesterday or last week), or, "I have finished a long letter to Father" (i.e., just now, but not yesterday or last week).

Some other examples, taken from Curme, will further illustrate this point. (Curme makes comparisons with the past tense, in giving his examples for the present perfect.)

"My brother bought two hats yesterday," but "My brother has bought two hats this week." (The week is not yet over. "My brother bought two hats this week" is, of course, also possible—as a representation of a past act.)

"I went to the theater last night," but "I *have been* ill all night, and do not feel like going to work this morning," since the speaker still feels the effects of the night's illness. If the speaker felt like working he would say, "I was ill all night, but I feel like working now" (the effects of the illness having worn off).

Curme also states that the present perfect can be used of time past ONLY where the person or thing in question still exists and the idea of past time is not prominent, i.e., where the reference is general or indefinite: "John has been punished many times" (general statement), but "John was punished many times last year" (definite). "I have been in England twice" (indefinite time).

This differentiation may become clearer in questions.

"Where were you an hour ago?" (yesterday, a week ago, a year ago, etc.).

"Where have you been?" (i.e., up to now, all day, or up to the present moment, all year, i.e., up to the present moment).

"Did you finish your work?" (i.e., an hour ago, yesterday, etc.).

"Have you finished your work?" (i.e., now, at this moment).

To SUM UP:

(1) Do NOT use the English perfect tense to describe action completed at a definite past time, i.e., hours or days or weeks ago. (2) Use the present perfect tense for past time actions that carry over into the present time, i.e., up to the present moment. The adverbial

particles just, recently, already, up to now, etc. all carry the past time actions forward into the present, and usually demand the present perfect tense. For example:

"I have (I've) just received your letter" (but, "I received your letter yesterday").

"I have recently made his acquaintance" (but, "I met him last week").

"I've already seen him" (but, "I saw him this morning").

CHAPTER XII

The Sequence of Tenses in Indirect Discourse
(Indirekte Rede)

IT IS only natural that Germans should have trouble with tenses in indirect discourse (after verbs of saying, believing, thinking, etc. in the main clause), because of a fundamental difference in German and English in the use of tenses in this construction. In German, the tense of the subordinate clause is often the tense that would have been used in direct discourse. Thus,

Er sagte, er sei reich (Er sagte, "Ich bin reich").
Er sagte, er werde bald kommen (Er sagte, "Ich werde bald kommen").

Also in indirect questions:

Er fragte ihn, wann er kommen werde. (Er fragte ihn: "Wann wirst du kommen?")
Er fragte ihn, was er getan habe. (Er fragte ihn: "Was hast du getan?") [1]

In English, there is an attraction of tenses (a sequence of tenses) in sentences like the above, which demands that, if the verb in the main clause is in the past tense, a past tense form be used in the subordinate (indirect discourse) clause. Thus,

He said he was sick (not he is sick).
He said he had once been rich (not he has once been rich).

---

[1] The German has other possibilities than the illustrations given, but in his wrong use of tenses in English in indirect discourse he is influenced by the examples cited.

He said he would come (not he will come).
He asked him when he was coming, or when he would come
(not when he is coming, or when he will come).
He asked him what he was doing (not what he is doing).
He asked him what he would do (not what he will do).[1]

AN EXCEPTION TO THIS RULE:

This sequence of tenses is not used, when the indirect statement
represents something as an habitual characteristic or permanently
or locally true. Thus,

They told us that the winters are cold in Vermont.
He asked me what the properties of acetylene are.
Sherman said that war is Hell.
Columbus believed that the earth is round.
The speaker said that honesty is the best policy.
I told him that the morning train leaves at nine.

---

[1] This sequence of tenses appears to be losing favor with careless speakers and
writers, but it should be carefully observed by Germans in speech and is considered
OBLIGATORY in good writing.

CHAPTER XIII

The Progressive Form
of the Verb

O F ALL the difficulties that confront a German learner of English, the correct use of the progressive is by common consent considered the greatest single difficulty. The German usually starts out by not using the progressive often enough, and then, when he becomes conscious of its frequency in English, he begins to use it "all over the place." Even German linguists, who have been in America for thirty or forty years and have achieved a sure Sprachgefühl for every other aspect of English, are baffled by the progressive. There are many reasons for this, several of which may be mentioned. (1) There is no equivalent German usage. (2) The average school grammar in Germany has a wholly inadequate treatment of it, and the American grammar usually attempts no explanation of its use. (3) The difficulty of presenting its correct use in precise words and in invulnerable examples. This last difficulty is due partly to the fact that frequently both the simple (or regular) form and the progressive can be used interchangeably or almost so, without any real difference in meaning, or with only such a slight difference as to defy adequate analysis within the compass of a few sentences. Whether it can be correctly and adequately defined and intelligibly illustrated by correct and incorrect examples, within the condensed form necessary for this book, only time will tell. But here goes.

DEFINITION OF THE PROGRESSIVE AND THE SIMPLE FORMS:

Curme, in his learned *Syntax,* enumerates the following differences between the verb in its *simple* form and its *progressive* form:

The progressive form stresses the conception of *continuation, repetition,* or *frequency.* The simple form expresses the idea of a *general* truth, an act as a *fact* or as a *whole,* or an act as *habitual, customary,* or *characteristic.* Curme, however, adds to his definition the statement that the simple form often implies the idea of duration, i.e., of a continuing action, but states that this conception is now never the leading one.

These definitions may serve as a point of departure for numerous examples, some of which will be taken from Curme. Thus,

Dogs *bark* is the characteristic act of dogs. "Dogs *are barking*" describes the act as now going on.

For some (to me) unaccountable reason, Curme quotes the sentence "I *live* (or *am living*) in Chicago" as "a habitual, customary act at the present time, often as here without an essential difference of meaning between the two forms." However, though these two forms might be interchangeable and express the same meaning, they may be used to conform exactly to the definitions given above. Thus,

"I *live* in Chicago" states the fact of my residence, my customary abode, my permanent residence, while "I *am living* in Chicago" implies a temporary residence, in other words, I haven't always lived in Chicago and I may not be living there next year or several years from now.

To illustrate this difference further: "I *live* in Chicago" is the answer to the question, "Where *do* you *live?*" The questioner's interest is in finding out your regular, permanent residence.

"I *am living* in Chicago is the answer to the question, "Where *are* you *living?*" (namely, now), with the questioner showing his interest in your present continuing residence, and implying that you have moved about a great deal and may move again within the not too distant future.

OTHER EXAMPLES:

The question "What *do* you *do?*" means that the questioner wants to know your customary employment, your job, your position, your life work. The answer to such a question is, "I *teach,*" namely, that is my occupation, "I am a teacher," or "I write," i.e., "I am a writer by profession."

The question "What *are* you *doing?*" implies What *are* you *doing* at the present time, and continuing to do at the present time, but not what your life work is. The answer to this question might be, "I *am writing,*" i.e., "I *am writing* a book, or a short story, though that isn't my normal activity; or "I *am teaching,*" i.e., I am teaching now, I used to do research work for the government, etc.

Amplifying this question may make this point stand out more clearly. "What *do* you *do* with yourself in the summer vacations?" implies that the questioner wants to know what your regular activity is in the summer months, where you take your vacations every summer, etc. The answers to this question might be, "I always *go* to Vermont in the summer," or "I always *do* research work in the summer."

"What *are* you *doing* with yourself this summer?" implies that the questioner believes that you may not have a customary activity in the summer or a customary summer residence and wants to know what particular activity you will indulge in the summer months, or where, among the many possibilities, you will spend your summer months, etc.

OTHER EXAMPLES:

"The town lies on a river" expresses a fact, a permanent situation. "The town is lying on the river" is quite impossible, unless the course of the river had been changed artificially. However, "The wounded man is still lying on the ground" (continuation, but not of course permanence).

Stylistic and Other Differences:

There are, however, other differences that do not fit so easily into the definition given above. "There he *comes*" is a mere statement of fact. "There he *is coming* down the road" is the descriptive, vivid way of putting it. This last example brings us to another concept that Curme has developed, which, taken together with his over-all definitions, is very helpful. He finds that the progressive is used instead of the simple form, to express a lively feeling of interest, expectancy, pleasure or displeasure, praise or censure, satisfaction or dissatisfaction, with the simple form merely registering the fact.

Examples of this (Curme's and my own) are the following:

1. "Recently John *has done* his work regularly" is the statement of fact, but
   "Recently John *has been doing* his work quite regularly" is the statement in a tone of praise and
   "Recently John *has been doing* his work very slovenly" is the statement in a tone of censure. "Recently John *has done* his work very slovenly" is the statement of fact, with *less* censure implied.

2. "We *shall* soon *have* plenty of rain" is the statement of fact or something so confidently expected that it is stated as a fact. We *shall* soon *be having* rain" (rain, and nothing but rain expresses displeasure at the thought of rain).

3. "We *are tramping* over the hills and *reading* and *writing* and *having* a restful time" is the lively description that implies pleasure and satisfaction.
   "We *tramp* over the hills and *read* and *write* and *have* a restful time" is the statement of the bare fact.

4. "I *was seeing* Nellie home, I *was seeing* Nellie home, and 'twas from Aunt Dinah's quilting party I *was seeing* Nellie home"; and "I *saw* Nellie home, I *saw* Nellie home, and 'twas

from Aunt Dinah's quilting party I *saw* Nellie home." I submit that the young man who *"was seeing* Nellie home" had a much better time than the young man who *"saw* Nellie home."

5. *"I'll be seeing* you" (the slangy American "Auf Wiedersehen") is spoken with much more warmth and interest and friendliness than the equally slangy but less warm *"I'll see* you again." (It is quite possible that the extra syllable in *seeing* and the high pitch of the syllable *see* in seeing help out in giving stress and pleasure to the idea of "Wiedersehen.")

6. "John *is bothering* me" has much more of complaint in it than "John *bothers* me," which is a statement of fact.

7. "How *are* you *feeling* this morning?" shows more sympathy and concern than "How *do* you *feel* this morning?" which just asks for the fact.

8. *"Are* you *leaving* for Chicago tomorrow?" expresses more friendly interest than the bare *"Do* you *leave* for Chicago tomorrow?"

In some of these examples, one may also feel the difference in time aspects, that is, the continuing action, continuing in the present and into the near future as against the idea of permanence, or customary action.

Misuse of the Progressive:

Some illustrations of the misuse of the progressive by Germans may clarify this discussion:

1. "I tell my students that all German weak nouns *are ending* in *n* in the plural." This sentence is wrong, because it is the *customary, habitual,* and *characteristic* thing for feminines to end in *n*. The sentence should read, "I tell my students that all weak nouns *end* in *n*," i.e., they always have ended in *n*, they always do end in *n*, and they always will end in *n*.

2. "All these old Babylonian documents *are employing* the Babylonian script." Since it was the established practice in

Babylonian manuscripts, this sentence must be corrected to "All these old Babylonian manuscripts *employ* the Babylonian script."

3. "These are good oranges. They *are coming* from California." If the dealer's oranges come from California regularly, this sentence is wrong. If the dealer wanted to stress the fact that he formerly sold Florida oranges, he could use a progressive with the adverb "now," thus, "My oranges are now coming from California" (they used to come from Florida).

4. "They are teaching the Humanities there just as they used to teach Kulturgeschichte in Germany" is wrong, if the writer is talking about the regular procedure in the teaching of the Humanities in a certain university, which is what this writer was doing. He could only justify his use of the progressive if this university had recently changed its method of teaching this course, in which case he would have written, "They are *now* teaching the Humanities, etc." with the implication that they formerly taught them differently.

5. "The children's reproduction of their parents' speech is deflected by the speech varieties they are hearing outside of the family." Since this is always and characteristically true of children, the sentence should be changed to read, "which they hear outside the family."

Wrong Use of the Simple Forms:

The sentence, "We now also *prepare* for a Xmas party," is not good, for a continuing action at the present moment is being stated and not a customary act. "We *are* now also *preparing* for a Xmas party" is the correct expression. Similarly, "Some of them *are trying* very hard already" should be used to describe an action continuing in the present rather than the incorrect "Some of them *try* very hard already."

CHAPTER XIV

English and German Word Order

THE usual sentence order in English is *subject first* and *verb second,* and departures from this order are relatively infrequent. For the German, who has much greater latitude in his placing of the subject (though the position of the verb is fixed), the adjustment to English word order causes many difficulties. Take the following examples: "Er kam gestern mit Karl," can be changed (except for the fixed second position of *kam*) to "Gestern kam er mit Karl" or "Mit Karl kam er gestern." The English translations of these three sentences are either "He came with Karl yesterday," or "Yesterday he came with Karl," but never "With Karl came he yesterday," or "Yesterday came he with Karl."

Germans must therefore guard themselves against their natural tendency to invert, i.e., to place some element of the sentence other than the subject before the verb. "Schoen siehst du heute aus," "Herrlich hat er gesungen," "Stark ist der Kerl," must all be translated into "You look lovely today," "He sang splendidly," "That fellow is very strong" (and never "Lovely look you," or "Lovely you look," or "Splendidly sang he," or "Splendidly he sang").

INVERSIONS IN ENGLISH:

Rare as inversions are in English, there are conditions under which they are, in the words of Fowler," [1] usual, desirable or per-

---

[1] Fowler, *Dictionary of Modern English Usage.*

missible." Some of these conditions will be noted here. Fowler lists them under the following rubrics:

1. *Negative Inversions* are possible and frequent both in conversation and in writing after such words as never, nor, scarcely, hardly, no sooner, little, seldom. Examples of this are:

    (*a*) Never was a decision more justified.

    (*b*) He isn't afraid, nor *am* I. Nor *do* I think that his opinion is relevant.

    (*c*) Hardly had we met, when he called me by my first name.

    (*d*) No sooner had I arrived, than he started to quarrel.

    (*e*) Little does he know about it.

    (*f*) Seldom have I met a finer fellow.

    (Except for *nor* which always demands inversion, these words can be placed in more "normal" positions. Thus, I have seldom met a finer fellow.)

2. *Hypothetical Inversion* (i.e., in conditional clauses):

    Were I he, I wouldn't do it. Had I known, I could have prevented it.

3. *Balance Inversion:* Among the guests were (long list).

4. *Link Inversion:* Next comes the question of pay. Now comes the difficulty.

5. *Signpost inversion:* By strategy is meant something wider.

Apart from these instances, which are frequent or common, inversion is rare in English. It still persists as a stylistic device for variation, but its frequent use is branded by Fowler "as one of the most repellent vices of modern writing." If used often by Germans it is sure to suggest German origin. It is of course widely found in the Bible, in the older literary language, and in poetry.

POSITION OF ADVERBS IN ENGLISH:

Learning these major rules for sentence word order does not clear up all the difficulties. There remains one outstanding difficulty, viz., the position of the adverb or of adverbs in English.

The matter would be simple, if one had definite rules for adverbial position in both English and German, but no such rules are available in either English or German handbooks. And the situation is not improved by the knowledge that in a single English sentence, the adverb may have one of three possible positions (the fourth position being the one the German might use). But as a point of departure, the following rule taken from Curme is very helpful:

An adverb can freely stand in almost any position *except between* a verb and its direct object, where its position is much less common than elsewhere. Thus one can say in English,
"*Yesterday* I met your father," or
"I met your father *yesterday*,"
but not
"I met *yesterday* your father," which is impossible, but is unfortunately the one position the German might choose in translating "Ich traf gestern deinen Vater."

OTHER EXAMPLES:

"He always (never, rarely) eats a big breakfast" for
"Er isst immer (nie, selten) ein grosses Frühstück" and not
"He eats seldom a big breakfast."
"He did his work first" or "He first did his work," but not
"He did first his work."

POSITION OF TWO ADVERBS, ONE OF TIME AND ONE OF PLACE:

"Er kam spät nach Hause," in which the adverb of time is first and the adverb of place second is the regular sequence in German. In English "He came home late" is the translation, and not "He came late home," which is impossible.

POSITION OF TWO ADVERBS, ONE OF PLACE AND ONE OF MANNER:

When an adverb of place and an adverb of manner are used in the same English sentence, the adverb of manner usually precedes the adverb of place. Thus, "He studies very hard at home," not "He studies at home very hard," unless one pauses after home.

Position of Two Adverbs, One of Time and One of Manner:

The adverb of manner usually precedes the adverb of time in the same English sentence. Thus "He worked very hard yesterday," and not "He worked yesterday very hard." The German "Er arbeitete gestern sehr fleissig" is responsible for the wrong word order in English.

Position of Three Adverbs, One of Time, One of Place, and One of Manner:

"He's studying very hard now at home" or "He's studying at home very hard now" are both possible, but normally not, "He's studying *now* very hard at home" or "He's studying *now* at home very hard."

Similarly: "He went to New York in his car yesterday" or "He went in his car to New York yesterday" are the usual possibilities, but not "He went yesterday in his car to New York" or "He went yesterday to New York in his car," which though not impossible are, for the Germans, the result of the influence of the German word order "Er fuhr gestern in seinem Wagen nach New York."

Summary:—Place the adverb of *time* after (and not before) the adverb or adverbs of *place* and *manner*.

Though this rule for the order of adverbs is a handy one, it does not explain the reasons behind these striking differences in German and English word order. These differences are the result of a different treatment of the complete verbal concept in German and in English. In English there is a strong tendency to keep the complete verbal concept close together, whereas Germans are accustomed to separating the verbal concept and stressing it in two places. To illustrate: Compare, "He *has seen* his friend" with "Er *hat* seinen Freund *gesehen."* Similarly, "He *must see* me this afternoon" and "Er *muss* mich heute nachmittag *besuchen."*

Applying this fundamental principle of word order to the examples already given, we find that in English one must say "He *came home* late" because *coming home* is the complete and inseparable verbal idea; on the other hand one usually says, in German, "Er kam spät nach Hause," putting the second part of the verbal idea in the position where one usually finds the second part of the verb. Compare, "Er kam spät zurück," *zurückkommen* being the complete verbal idea. This explanation of the differences between English and German word order is an application of the late Professor Erich Drach's study of *Grundgedanken der deutschen Satzlehre.*

POSITION OF INDIRECT AND DIRECT OBJECTS:

"Er gab seinem Freunde das Buch" is translatable as "He gave his friend the book." However, if instead of "his friend" one says "to his friend," the order is changed to "He gave the book to his friend," and not "He gave to his friend the book." But if a restrictive relative clause is added, e.g., "he asked for," the order is "He gave (to) his friend the book he asked for."

POSITION OF COMPOUND VERBS:

Be careful with such compound verbs as get up, try on, eat up, put on, go down, etc. It might be a good practice for a German to avoid all difficulties by always keeping them together. Thus,

I *get up* early in the morning.

I *tried on* my suit.

I *ate up* my cereal.

I *put on* my coat.

The sun *goes down* at six o'clock.

Some of these verbal combinations may be separated by a word or two, e.g.,

I tried my suit on.
I ate my cereal up.
I put my coat on.
(but "I *get* early in the morning *up,* and "The sun *goes* at six o'clock *down*" are absolutely impossible.)

CHAPTER XV

Abridgment of Clauses to Phrases and Words

A CHARACTERISTIC phenomenon of the English language is its ability to contract subordinate clauses to infinitive, participial, and gerundial phrases. Since this can be done only to a very limited extent in German, and since the uncontracted clauses usually constitute good English, Germans are slow to make use of this time-saving device. However, the abridgments are so idiomatic and so characteristic of English that they should be cultivated. Moreover, they are almost without exception acceptable in both informal and formal English, and the absence of them is likely to attract attention, particularly when the uncontracted clauses are awkward, as they frequently are, having therefore been superseded by the abridgments.

The abridgments listed below are arranged in definite groups that follow Curme's treatment of them in his *Syntax* (*Grammar of the English Language*), and the nomenclature is Curme's as well as many of the examples. The abridgments that are identical with German usage are not listed.

Abridgment of Relative Clause:

The time has come (at which) to speak out. (The time has come at which we must speak out.)

Abridgment of Subject Clause:

His losing out in the competition did not surprise us. (That he lost out in the competition, did not surprise us.)

Abridgment of Genitive Clause:

I reminded him of his having promised it. (I reminded him that he had promised it.)

Abridgment of Dative Clause:

He is unkind to all opposing him. (He is unkind to whoever opposes him.)

Abridgment of Accusative Clause:

I desire the rubbish to be removed. (I desire that the rubbish be removed.)

I cannot help expressing my fears. (The uncontracted clause is impossible.)

Abridgment of Clause of Time:

Driving home, we ran into a heavy fog. (When we drove home we ran into a heavy fog.)

When young, I did such things differently. (When I was young, I did such things differently.)

Before going down town, I met an old friend. (Before I went down town, I met an old friend.)

After having finished (finishing) our studies we turned on the radio. (After we had finished our studies, we turned on the radio.)

Abridgment of Clause of Manner Proper:

I beat him playing in our match. (I beat him, as I played in our match—which is clumsy.)

Abridgment of Manner Clauses of Modal Result and Pure Result:

He got the car going (running) again. (He got the car so that it ran again.)

Abridgment of Clause of Cause:

Seeing no filling station anywhere, we drove on to the next town. (Since we saw no filling station anywhere, we drove on to the next town.)

Being sick, I just couldn't come. (Since I was sick, I just couldn't come—this is a bit awkward.)

Having made the same mistakes, I know what you suffered. (Since I've made the same mistakes, I know what you suffered.)

Owing to his bringing me word so late, I couldn't go. (Owing to the fact that he brought me word so late, I couldn't go—this is a bit awkward.)

Abridgment of the Clause of Condition or Exception:

Strictly speaking, that is not true. (If one must speak strictly, that is not true—this is awkward.)

Judging by his looks, he won't live long. (If one judges by his looks, he won't live long. Strict grammarians sometimes object to the abridged clause, but it is in good usage.)

Excepting a few mistakes, I think he writes English very well. (If one excepts, or, If I except a few mistakes, I think he writes English very well.)

Abridgment of Concessive Clause:

Conceding his superiority as a scholar, it is evident that he is inferior as a man. (Even if one concedes his superiority as a scholar, it is evident that he is inferior as a man.)

Abridgment of Clause of Means:

By holding on to the rope firmly, we got to the shore safely. (An idiomatic unabridged clause for this is virtually impossible.)

Additional Examples Listed Without Being Classified:

We saw them coming out of the restaurant.

Going by train, you'll get there much sooner.

We thought their turning around showed that they knew us.

Occupying your mind with such matters won't help you.

A man bringing such news is always welcome.

I saw her trying on all the hats in the store and forgetting all
about supper.

There's nothing doing. (Slang)

Her bowing sweetly to me, doesn't mean a thing.

She dressed as though trying to imitate Marlene Dietrich.

He was accused of being dishonest.

He was prevented from coming by having a bad cold.

He differed from other boys of his age in having good manners.

He was reported as having lost all his money.

She always chews gum (when) riding in the subway.

You ought to have told me, instead of my telling you.

Liking him so much, I could recommend him highly.

He enlisted without his parents' knowing about it.

Recapitulation:

These abridgments *must* be cultivated both in speech and writing. They are in the spirit and genius of the English language
and though many of the unabridged clauses are just as good, many
others are hopelessly clumsy or awkward. The German can contract some subordinate clauses, but he is much more limited in
his possibilities. He might contract many of the above clauses into
nouns, which is also possible in English. But such contractions lose
the verbal effect and are, therefore, often less forceful.

CHAPTER XVI

Eliminating Flickwörter
in English
"Already Once Again"

THE German can pile up Flickwörter both in speaking and writing to a degree that is impossible in English. He can say quite naturally and commonly, "Da hat er's schon wieder mal gemacht," thus using four adverbial particles in a short sentence. The English translation of this sentence is, "He's done it again," which, if spoken with the proper stresses and inflection of the voice, renders the German exactly. The German can even use a sentence with five Flickwörter in conversation, e.g., "Da hat der Kerl heute doch schon wieder mal mehr getan (als man von ihm erwartete. Das ist allerhand"). In English this sentence will read, "That fellow's done more again today," with a reduction of five Flickwörter to one, and of six adverbs to two. "Da bin ich halt wieder mal ausgegangen" is sufficiently translated by "Then I went out again," with a reduction of three particles to one.

Translating sentences such as these into such monstrosities in English as, "He's done it already once again," does violence to the English language. This "already once again" combination appears so frequently in the English speech of Germans that Americans employ it in humorous imitations of their speech. It needs therefore to be watched. With a little practice Germans will be surprised to find that these words rarely need to be used in English, if their meaning can be indicated by the context and the proper intonation and stress. "Schon wieder einmal" is not the only dangerous combination. One must beware of using, with anything like their German frequency, the translations of the German *auch*, *noch*, *doch*, *wohl*, *schon*, *sogar*, *wieder*, *immer*, *gerade*, *gleichfalls*, *sozusagen*. There are, of course, English equivalents of these words, such as, *also*, *yet*, *still*, *probably*, *well*, *so really*, *generally*, *to be sure*, *just*, etc., but they are relatively infrequent. Aronstein in his *Englische Stilistik* gives several sentences in German and English, which further illustrate this point.

Ich darf *auch* nicht vergessen, dass wir an Bord der Yacht stiegen.	I must not forget that we went on board the yacht.
Ich habe *noch* heute Besuch zu erwarten.	I am expecting a visitor tonight.
"Man muss *ja* keine Zeit versäumen," sagte sie.	"We mustn't lose time," she said.
Ein Grad der Bildung, der *eigentlich* keinem Manne fehlen sollte.	A degree of refinement no man ought to be without.

(In this last sentence *really* could be added—"A degree of refinement no man *really* ought to be without," but the addition of *really* does not make the statement stronger.)

The use of these and similar adverbs should also be closely watched in serious writing. The careful writer of English finds it much less necessary to use so-called "hook and eye words," which unite one sentence with another, than the German. German prose is likely to be studded with such words as allein, hingegen, denn, nun, so, indessen. Their English equivalents, e.g., however, on the other hand, etc., may appear fairly frequently in closely reasoned scientific writing, but in ordinary prose they can often be entirely dispensed with.

NOTE: There is a marked tendency among modern German writers to reduce the number of "Flickwörter" and "hook and eye" words.

CHAPTER XVII

Difficulty with Some Common Usages

WHEN to use *that* and *which* in relative clauses: Fowler, in his *Modern English Usage,* which many teachers and writers look upon as the last word in usage, suggests that *that* be used in defining (restrictive clauses) and *which* in nondefining (explanatory) clauses, thus,

> (*a*) Each made a list of the books *that* had influenced him (restrictive).
>
> (*b*) I always buy his books, *which* have influenced me greatly (explanatory).

In typically Fowlerian manner, he adds that "it would be idle to pretend that it is the practice either of most or of the best writers." After such a statement, Germans need not worry greatly about the problem, but if they want a rule, Fowler's is as good as any.

It should be noted, however, that this rule does not provide a completely satisfactory differentiation. Three concrete examples that illustrate differences in *that* and *which* may prove helpful.

THE USE OF THAT AND WHICH:

1. Use *which* and not *that* in the following restrictive clause: The books of *which* I spoke are not in the library. *That* is impossible after a preposition in a relative clause.
2. Two *thats* in close proximity in the main and relative clauses are usually avoided for the sake of euphony, or style. Thus, People like to do *that which* they do well, and not *that that* they do well.

3. *Which* must be used in a relative clause like the following: I went out in the pouring rain without my rubbers, *which* was a very foolish thing to do. (If *that* were used for *which* in this sentence, it would change the relative clause to an independent sentence.)

The Use of CAN for MAY:

Though strict grammarians insist on the proper differentiation between *can* and *may* (*können* und *dürfen*) *can* is now well established in cultivated colloquial usage. Thus, "Can I go now?" appears to have taken the place of "May I go now?" to such an extent that "May I go now" is beginning to sound somewhat stilted or consciously grammatical.

The Translation of the German "Man":

There is no single equivalent for the very useful German *"man."* The English *one* cannot be used with anything like the same frequency as *man*. There are several possible translations for the German sentence, "Man macht das nicht in Amerika." They are, "One doesn't do that in America," "We don't do that in America," "That isn't done in America," "People don't do that in America," "You don't do that in America." It is difficult to say what order of preference should be given to these possibilities. However, "One doesn't do that in America" would be well down toward the bottom of the list, at least in conversational speech.

The usual translation of "Man sagt" is "It is said" and not "One says," and for the sentence "Man sagt, dass er steinreich ist," the translations are not "One says that he is very rich," but "He is said to be very rich," or "They say he is very rich," with the second sentence being the more informal of the two.

The Teacher Was Given a Book:

Germans, who think much more grammatically than Americans, find it difficult to use such completely idiomatic but apparently ungrammatical sentences as, "The teacher was given a book by his admiring students." They need, therefore, to acquire the feeling for this strange construction, as well as for others that seem equally ungrammatical, e.g., "He was presented with a loving cup."

I Am Afraid:

The "I am afraid" combinations do valiant service in informal speech and writing for a large variety of German expressions. While in such an expression as, "I'm afraid it's going to rain," they may express the same amount of fear that is expressed in "Ich fürchte, es gibt Regen," there is usually no connotation of fear in most of its uses. Thus, in the answer to an invitation, "I'm afraid we can't come," "I'm afraid" suggests "We'd like to come, but the chances are against our coming." It is thus also a form of regret. The rejection of an article for publication may be couched in the words, "I'm afraid we cannot publish your article," and is a hundred per cent rejection, which may sound less blunt than the more formal, "We are sorry that we cannot publish your article." If in a crowded train your seat-mate has gone to the diner and a passenger asks you, "Is this seat taken?" your answer might well be, "I'm afraid it is," which again is very definite information, but more graciously expressed than in "Yes, it is," or in "Yes, I believe it is." The frequent use of "I'm afraid" is therefore recommended.

CHAPTER XVIII

Current Established American English Usage Sometimes Objected to by Purists

ABOUT ten years ago, the late Professor S. A. Leonard of the University of Wisconsin questionnaired seven groups of Americans in an effort to determine the acceptability or non-acceptability of many words and phrases. Included in these groups were four groups of teachers, linguists, English teachers, members of the Modern Language Association, and speech teachers; and three nonacademic groups, authors, business men, and editors. On the basis of his answers, he classified the words and phrases as established, disputable, and illiterate. Some of his conclusions are presented in this chapter.

Since Germans cannot use disputed words with the same feeling of authority which native Americans might have, only the words and phrases that are ESTABLISHED are listed here:

1. They invited my friends and *myself* (established, but not by a large majority).
2. This is the chapter *whose* contents cause most discussion. (The use of *whose* in the place of the pedantic *of which* established.)
3. None of them *are* here (*are* established instead of the grammatically correct but pedantic *is*).
4. Everyone was here, but *they* all went home early (*everyone* synonymous with *all*).
5. It is *me* (established).

6. If it *wasn't* for football, school life would be dull (*wasn't* for *weren't* established as good colloquial usage).

7. We can expect the commission *to at least protect* our interests (the *split infinitive* established).

8. The invalid was able *partially to raise* his body (established as correct but stilted. In other words, the split infinitive is often preferable to the "unsplit" infinitive).

9. We will *try and* get it (established as perfectly correct for cultivated colloquial use. Similarly, "come *and* get it." The use of *and* instead of *to* has been literary English for centuries).

10. I will go, *providing* you keep away (established as as acceptable as *provided*).

11. Harry was a little shaver about *this* tall (*this* established for *so* in cultivated colloquial English).

12. Our catch was *pretty* good (established as cultivated colloquialism as a synonym for *rather* and *fairly*).

13. (a) That's a dangerous curve, you'd better go *slow*.
   (b) Drive *slow* down that hill.
   (c) My father walked very *slow* down the street.
   (*Slow* for *slowly* safely established as adverb in all three sentences, with however strong protest against *slow* in the third sentence, because it is followed by a phrase.)

14. We *only* had one left (the pre-auxiliary position of *only* established).

15. I felt I could walk no *further* (*further* for *farther* established in spite of grammar rule).

16. A treaty was concluded *between* the four powers (established as better than *among*, for *between* can express the relationship of a thing to surroundings both severally and individually, whereas *among* expresses a relation to them collectively and vaguely).

17. He stood *in front* of the class (*in front of* for *before* established by almost unanimous rating).

18. The catcher stands *back of* home plate (omission of preposition *in*, and *back of* established).

19. He doesn't do it *the way* I do (established).

20. He came *around* four o'clock (established).

21. He did not do *as* well *as* we expected (first *as* instead of the *so* required by many grammars, established).

22. I don't know *if* I can (*if* for *whether* established by a five-eighths vote).

23. (a) I *had rather* go at once.

(b) You had *better* stop that foolishness. (Both established.)

24. My *folks* sent me a check (*folks* as preferable to *people* established).

25. I've absolutely *got* to go (*got* for *have* established as acceptable colloquialism).

26. I have *got* my own opinion on that (established as colloquial).

27. This room is *awfully* cold (*awfully* established as having moved from slang into cultivated English).

28. He made *a date* for next week (established as having moved from slang into accepted informal speech).

29. Have you *fixed* the fire for the night? (established as cultivated colloquial English in the United States).

30. I *guess* I'll go to lunch (safely established as informal American English. Classically good English in England, which has become obsolete there and is now condemned as illiterate or as an Americanism by British linguists).

CHAPTER XIX

American Slang,
Its Use and Abuse

SLANG as one of the most striking phenomena of American speech deserves mention in this book, but it needs first to be defined. Greenough and Kittredge, in *Words and Ways in English Speech,* define it as a "peculiar kind of vagabond language, always hanging on the outskirts of legitimate speech, but continually straying or forcing its way into the most respectable company . . . in fact slang may almost be called the only living language, the only language in which these processes (growth of language) can be seen in full activity." This definition gives to slang a unique place as a creative, life-giving force in the growth and change of language. But another sentence needs to be added: While many slang words "stray or force" their way into respectable company, many more lead a short, fitful existence and soon pass into oblivion.

It is only natural that many Germans in America should soon be lost in admiration of American slang, for there is a colorfulness, picturesqueness, and aptness about much of it that appeals to all but pedants and purists. It has even attracted high praise from the conservative British, many of whom have been schooled to frown on Americanisms. Illustrative of this are the words of E. C. Bentley, the English editor of Damon Runyon, one of the slangiest American writers: "We [the English] produce little slang of our own: what we have that is English is of old standing. Our borrowing [of American slang] is, I suppose, one of the results of the enormous impression made on us (whether we like it or not) by the vigor, the vivacity, the originality, the drama and melodrama of American life."

All this means that Germans in America must familiarize themselves with American slang, if they want to understand American English and American life, and surely one of the final tests of their command of their new language is their sovereign use of its slang. But there are pitfalls for the unwary foreigner who uses slang indiscriminately, and a few words of caution are necessary. In the first place, as has been already said, many slang words are too ephemeral in nature to enjoy general acceptability, even as slang, and should therefore be avoided. But more important are some other considerations. There are several kinds of slang. There is the slang of particular social groupings; there is the slang of the baseball field, soldier slang, sailor slang, student slang, movie and theater slang, Broadway slang, underworld slang, to mention only a few. Though some of the slang from each of these groups may be generally comprehensible in all the groups, much of it is not, and a German who is not a member of any of these groups must know what is generally acceptable, before using slang. He should also attempt to adhere to a fairly uniform pattern in his slang. In addition, each age group has its own peculiar slang; there is the slang of the adolescents, the slang of college students, the slang of young men and women, and the slang of the older generations. For German parents to adopt the slang of their adolescent American-schooled children may produce utterly undignified and ludicrous effects. To take a very harmless example: "O.K." is probably the only word that most school and college students use for "All right," but it has not yet forced its way into the speech of the older generations in cultured professional groups. When therefore a middle-aged dignified German professor, doctor, or lawyer uses it exclusively in his otherwise rather stilted, overly careful English, the effect is unconsciously humorous. (O.K. as a technical term in approving printer's copy or reports is generally accepted.) The best advice that can be given to Germans is to adopt only such slang as is current in their age, social, and professional groups.

CHAPTER XX

American English and British English

FOR Germans who began their study of English in German schools and were, therefore, taught British English and a contempt for American English, the psychological and practical adjustment to American English is not easy. But the problem should not provide too many difficulties. It should be said at the outset that there is no choice left for the Germans in America but to give up both their British accent, or their near British accent, and their specifically British vocabulary. For the few who speak this English flawlessly this means a considerable sacrifice, since these few, proud of their mastery of what appears to them to be a superior brand of English, both in pronunciation and in choice of words, will hold tenaciously to it. By so doing they may enjoy being flattered by being taken for Englishmen, but they will remain foreigners in America, although the foreignism of Englishmen is for obvious reasons less objectionable than the foreignism of Germans. However, for the vast majority of Germans who have never succeeded wholly in learning British English perfectly, the adjustment to American English involves giving up very little.

Apart from the importance of doing in Rome as the Romans do, there is one other reason that should influence Germans to accept American English as the authoritative brand in America, namely, the changed trend in usage, which many trained observers are now noticing. A generation or two ago, British English was accepted by many Americans as the standard English. Englishmen felt that they were the guardians of good English and fought vigorously against Americanisms, or accepted them only with the greatest reluctance. The situation today is quite different. Americans no longer accept the imprimatur of England in the matter of choice of words or their usage. Established usage in America is good enough for them, regardless of what Englishmen feel about it. And the British today, much as they may inwardly protest against peculiarly American expressions, are consciously and unconsciously accepting increasingly large numbers of them into their body of English. For this shift in the development of English, the tremendous popularity of the American movies, of American phonograph records, American sheet music, the American radio, and, of course, the ever-increasing importance of America, are responsible. It is quite unlikely that this trend will be reversed in the immediate or distant future; all of which means that Germans studying English need not shy away from good Americanisms, except possibly when they are writing for British consumption only.

There are three kinds of differences between British English and American English.

1. The difference in vocabulary.
2. The difference in pronunciation and speech tune.
3. The difference in spelling.

The Difference in Vocabulary:

It is the current fashion to overemphasize the differences in vocabulary in use in Britain and America. Henry L. Mencken's 800-page book, *The American Language,* and the *Dictionary of American English,* now being edited at the University of Chicago, have contributed to this overemphasis. There are, of course, a tremendous number of words that are used in Britain which are not current in America, and vice versa, and also a large number of words that are used with wholly different meanings, or with different shades of meaning, in the two countries. A comprehensive listing of such words would reach impressive proportions and supply what seems to be conclusive evidence of the importance of these differences. However, in spite of many differences in household and technical terms and in current colloquialisms, there remains an overwhelming preponderance of words in common use in these two great streams of current English. Literary English in Britain and America, though not wholly identical, is still in such close agreement that only the trained philologist, or an Englishman with a strong scent for Americanisms, or a decreasing number of Americans who prefer Briticisms to Americanisms, can differentiate between two literary passages of British and American English. The war speeches of Franklin D. Roosevelt and Winston Churchill are understood in both America and Britain in the precise meanings of the language these two statesmen give to their thoughts, for there is little in their speeches that is either peculiarly American or peculiarly British. American and British poets and novelists, except when they make use of colloquialisms and dialect, have essentially the same vocabulary, which is their common heritage of English from Shakespeare down to the present day. American and British historians, economists, philologists, philosophers, natural scientists, editorial writers and publicists generally, use this common heritage, and good American English style is thus good British English style, and vice versa.

A German may find a parallel to this whole phenomenon in the differences in German between the German of the cultured Austrian and the German of the cultured German of the "Reich." Stripped of Austrian and Reich colloquialisms and a fairly impressive list of expressions for household furnishings, etc., the common language is virtually identical in both countries, and differences between these two types of German, particularly in literary German, if distinguishable at all, are usually distinguishable only by trained philologists.

SOME DIFFERENCES IN PRONUNCIATION:

To enumerate all the differences between British and American pronunciation would exceed the limits set for this book. Comments on a few general and specific differences may, however, be helpful.

There are two fairly major differences, namely in the vowel quality of the *o* and the *a*. The British short *o* in such words as box and hot is still definitely a short *o* sound, while the American *o* in such words is the same *a* sound that the German has in "sagen." The *a* sound in such words as bath, path, half, past, wrath is spoken by the British with an *ah* sound, whereas most Americans, except for many New Englanders and Americans on the Eastern seaboard, give these words approximately the same sound the German uses in the umlauted *ä*.

The British have a tendency to reduce syllables with secondary stress to unstressed syllables, and unstressed syllables to virtually nothing. Thus such words as dictionary, stationery, library, which in American English have two clearly marked stresses, one a primary and the other a secondary stress, become, when spoken by a Briton, dikshnri, stāshnri, libri. This tendency affects a large number of words and clearly differentiates the two nationalities.

Other differences in commonly used words are in the words schedule, lieutenant, laboratory, which the British pronounce as shedule, leftenant, labórtri, and the Americans skedule, liutenant, láboratóry.

Differences in Speech Tune:

Though there is a fairly close resemblance between British and American speech tune in its major aspects, as is evidenced in the general speech tunes of Roosevelt and Churchill, and of British American and British broadcasters, there are many subtle differences particularly in colloquial speech, too many to be given here. One difference should, however, be mentioned, the difference in the melody of the question. In the question, "Have you been there?" the American starts his question in a low note, raises his voice to its high point on *been* and then drops it slightly on *there*. The Briton starts out on a high pitch on *Have you,* lowers his pitch on *been* and raises it on *there*. This difference in the inflection of the voice in questions is great enough to differentiate an Englishman from an American, even if every other aspect of his speech were identical.

SOME DIFFERENCES IN SPELLING:

An actual count of words spelled differently in Britain and America reaches impressive proportions, but on the basis of frequency the number is not very great. A few of these differences in commonly used words should, however, be noted. The difference which strikes the eye most is the prevailing British practice to spell such words as honor, labor, behavior, rigor, endeavor, candor, and others, as honour, labour, behaviour, rigour, endeavour, candour. The British justify their *our* spelling of these words on the ground that they were originally loan words from the French. Though it has been proved that they are inconsistent in this practice, since they use *or* in many other words that came into the English language from the French, such as mirror, governor, they are so sensitive on this point that American publishers sometimes use the *our* spelling in order to ensure a sale for their books in England. This difference therefore remains the outstanding single difference. Americans have adopted the British *our* spelling only in the word the Saviour, using the *or* spelling, however, when it is not capitalized, savior.

Among the differences in other common words are (with the American spelling given first) caliber—calibre, center—centre, fiber—fibre, theater—theatre, liter—litre, cider—cyder, siphon—syphon, siren—syren, automobile tire—automobile tyre, check—cheque, czar—tsar, gray—grey, jail—gaol, program—programme.

CHAPTER XXI

Differences in Punctuation Between English and German

KIERZEK in the *Macmillan Handbook of English* prefaces his rules for the use of the comma with the following sentence: "The student who expects a rule for every possible use of the comma is like the boy who buys a handbook of correspondence in order to find out what he should write to his sweetheart." This sentence not only expresses picturesquely a common-sense view on the use of commas in English, but also illustrates strikingly, by its total absence of commas, essential differences between their use in English and German. A German following his Duden or some other standard reference book would punctuate this sentence in German as follows: Der Student, der eine Regel für jeden möglichen Gebrauch des Kommas erwartet, ist gleich dem jungen Mann, der einen Liebesbriefsteller kauft, um herauszufinden, was er seinem Mädchen schreiben soll—thus using five commas to none in English.

Though English and German grammars state the function of punctuation identically (namely, the function of punctuation is to make clear the meaning of the written language), there are considerable differences between English and German, particularly in the use of the comma, the exclamation point, and the colon. In general, Germans, following Duden's "feste Regeln," punctuate far more frequently than Americans, who have fewer "feste Regeln," and are allowed greater freedom. While educated Germans will probably punctuate the same passages identically, educated Americans will differ among themselves. Moreover they punctuate freely or less freely, according as they write for different sets of readers, using many commas when writing for small children or adolescents, and fewer when writing for highly educated readers.

THE COMMA:

The following examples will illustrate some of the major differences in punctuation between German and English:

1. The German normally separates all complete clauses, whether co-ordinate or subordinate, by commas. There is no such fast rule for clauses in English. In long co-ordinate clauses, commas are used in English, but they are usually omitted in short compound sentences, such as, "I looked back on my youth and I recalled many happy experiences."

2. German Nebensätze introduced by dass, als, wenn, weil, etc. are always separated by commas. In English, commas are demanded when the subordinate clauses are long, or for the sake of clarity, but they are usually omitted in short sentences. Thus,

He is older than he looks.	Er ist älter, als er aussieht.
When I go to the theater I want to be entertained.	Wenn ich ins Theater geh, will ich mich amüsieren.
He said that he was sorry.	Er sagte, dass es ihm leid tue.
He was there when I came.	Er war schon da, als ich kam.
That the enemy was beaten was only too clear.	Dass der Feind geschlagen war, war nur zu klar.

3. The rule for commas in English relative clauses is the most important to learn. Whereas in German one sets off all relative clauses by commas, in English one uses commas ONLY before so-called explanatory relative clauses and NEVER before so-called restrictive relative clauses (einschränkende Relativsätze). This rule is important and must be observed.

EXAMPLES OF RESTRICTIVE RELATIVE CLAUSES:

The German who desires to speak English well has a lot to learn.

He brought me the fruit which was lying on the table.

The man who spoke to us was a close friend.

Examples of Explanatory or Non-Restrictive Relative Clauses:

My English teacher, who doesn't know any German, has great difficulty in explaining the differences between English and German.

My mother, who belongs to the older generation, disapproves of the younger generation.

4. Infinitive phrases beginning with the English equivalents of um, zu, ohne zu, anstatt zu (in order to, without, instead of) are not set off by commas.

I never came home without bringing you something.

Ich kehrte niemals heim, ohne euch etwas mitzubringen.

Do you expect to win the great prize in the lottery?

Hoffst Du, das grosse Los zu ziehen?

5. A rather important difference in the use of commas occurs in enumerations (Aufzählungen). If the words in the series are unconnected by *and,* there is no difference. Thus,

Men, women, children met in the market place.

But if the words are united by *and,* the comma is dropped in German, but retained in English, according to some handbooks. Thus,

Men, women, and children met in the market place.

However, many authorities permit the omission of the comma before *and.* Thus,

Men, women and children met in the market place.

The Exclamation Point:

The exclamation point is used much less in English than in

German. American handbooks of English caution against its over-use, and ask for commas or periods after mild interjections. The fact that there is no single symbol for the exclamation point on standard American typewriters, and that three separate manipulations are necessary to produce it, is sufficient evidence of its relative unimportance. American girls in their teens may intersperse their letters with exclamation points, but adult Americans avoid them, except to express a very high degree of surprise, incredulity, or other strong emotion.

EXAMPLES:

But as for me, give me liberty or give me death!	Strong emotion.
Forbid it, Almighty God!	Strong emotion.
Oh, how can you say that?	Mild emotion.
Well, what do you say now?	Mild emotion.
Close the door.	Mild command.
Close the door!	Strong command.

THE COLON:

The chief difference between the English and German use of the colon is before direct quotations. In German every direct quotation is preceded by a colon, whereas in English SHORT (and that means most) quotations are preceded by commas. For example, Tom said, "We'll drive along the road." Colons are seldom used in the punctuation of dialogues in American novels and plays, and are used only to introduce long and formal quotations.

CHAPTER XXII

Syllabication and Trennsilben

WORDS at the end of a line, whether in printing, typewriting, or handwriting, are divided less frequently in English than in German. There are several reasons for this, three of which deserve to be mentioned. (1) English words are as a rule shorter than German words. The relative shortness of many common English words as compared to German words reduces the need for division both in printing and in writing, and also facilitates spacing between words. Compare, e.g., these common English words and their German equivalents. I—ich, a—ein, einen, this—dieser, or—oder, had—hatte, lost—verloren, set—gesetzt, made—gemacht, few—wenige. (2) The compound character of many German words makes divisions between the compounded elements obvious and avoids the confusion that often results from divisions in English words. (3) The German rule of dividing a word by Sprechsilben, and not Sprachsilben, has no counterpart in English, which divides either by Sprech- or Sprachsilben. Thus in German one divides Heizung, Hei-zung, Vertretung, Ver-tre-tung, as Sprechsilben, whereas in English one divides fiction, fiction (Sprechsilbe), but heat-ing, lik-ing (Sprachsilben). Such apparent inconsistency is puzzling not only to the German but to the American as well. But the problem is not really a serious one, as anyone who consults English handbooks may learn. Very little space is devoted to it in these handbooks, and that little space consists largely of two admonitions:

1. Avoid dividing a word at the end of a line.
2. When in doubt about dividing, consult your dictionary, which will indicate the syllable divisions.

Dividing syllables in English is therefore largely the problem of the printer, who will, in deciding where to divide, consult the dictionary and follow whatever rules for syllabication are set down in such standard Style Manuals as those published by the U.S. Government Printing Office and the University of Chicago Press or in the style manual of his own printing establishment.

The typist, who is under no necessity of creating a blocked page, may nevertheless, for appearance's sake, sometimes have to divide. For him a few obvious rules are given in English handbooks in addition to the all important admonition of "consult the dictionary." *Harbrace Handbook of English* lists only four.

1. Never divide a word to set off a single letter: e-nough, a-gainst, man-y are wrong.

2. Never confuse the reader by setting off an -ed pronounced as part of the preceding syllable: enjoy-ed, remember-ed are wrong.

3. Divide hyphenated words only at the hyphen. A second hyphen is awkward: fire-eat-er is wrong.

4. Never divide a word of a single syllable: sla-ve, lea-ve are wrong.

The German who writes by hand (script) has all his problems eliminated, for many Americans get along without ever dividing a word in script, and Germans may follow their example with impunity.

CHAPTER XXIII

An Important Hint
on Learning English

DON'T take the comments of Americans on the beautiful way you speak English too seriously. Americans, who as compared to Germans are poor linguists, are likely, both in sincere admiration and in a spirit of friendliness and flattery, to speak only in praise of your acquisition of English, and never of course to correct your mistakes, UNLESS YOU INSIST UPON IT OVER AND OVER AGAIN. The result is that there are many highly educated Americans of German birth who, after thirty or forty years in America, are daily guilty of crass Germanisms in their speech, all because none of their colleagues or friends ever called their attention to them. Such a thing would be impossible in Germany, where foreigners, even those who speak German fairly well, are continually informed and reminded of the mistakes they are making, usually in a very friendly but direct manner, e.g., "Das können Sie nicht sagen," or "Wir sagen das so." Few Americans, even when they know Germans intimately, will of their own accord call attention to mistakes.

It follows from this that Germans who want to learn to speak and write English well, or flawlessly, must cultivate American friends and insist on the correction of their mistakes. These American friends should be preferably not only native-born Americans, but those whose Sprachgefühl can be presumed to be correct. Such Americans may not always be able to tell you why your English is wrong, but they will know what you should have said.

A WORD OF CAUTION:

Don't let such American friends tell you that your English speech is guttural and that you must speak farther to the front of your mouth. Except for the *ach* sound, the guttural *r,* and the guttural glottal stop (Kehlkopfverschlusslaut), German enunciation is much farther to the front of the mouth than English, and Germans in their English must produce sounds farther back in the mouth, AWAY FROM the teeth and the tip of the tongue, and NOT NEARER them.

CHAPTER XXIV

Common Errors of Germans in Speaking and Writing English

One Hundred Examples— With Corrections

THE errors listed in this chapter were not manufactured for this book. They are all authentic examples, for which I am indebted to many German friends and acquaintances. In some cases, the reasons for the corrections are given, in others, the reasons may be found in the chapters on Tenses, Word Order, etc. Errors in punctuation have also been corrected.

WRONG USE OF TENSES:

1. Some of them try very hard already.
   Correct: Some of them are trying very hard (already).
   I go to the store now.
   Correct: I'm going to the store now.
   We also prepare for a Christmas party.
   Correct: We are also preparing for a Christmas party.
2. I go down town tomorrow.
   I telephone him next week.
   Correct: I'm going down town tomorrow, or I'll go down town tomorrow.
   I'm going to telephone him, or I'll telephone him.
   (If these sentences stand alone and are not answers to such

questions as, "When do you go down town?" or "When are you going down town?" etc., the simple present tense form should not be used with a future meaning. Only after such questions as, "When do you sail?" "When do you leave (are you leaving) for Chicago?" can the simple present with a future meaning be justified. Thus as answers to questions like the above, it is correct to say, "I sail tomorrow," "I leave tomorrow on the 4:40." The future forms are used less frequently in answer to such questions.)

So I think, I give up the idea for this summer.

Correct: So I think I'll give up the idea for this summer.

It is very hot here and I am glad when I get back to the farm.

Correct: It is very hot here and I'll be glad when I get back to the farm.

3. I tell my students that all weak nouns are ending in *n* in the plural.

Correct: I tell my students that all weak nouns end in *n* in the plural.

They are good oranges. They are coming from California.

Correct: They come from California.

They are teaching there Humanities just as they taught in old Germany Kulturgeschichte.

Correct: They teach the Humanities there just as they taught Kulturgeschichte in old Germany.

Children's reproduction of *the* parents' speech is deflected by the speech varieties they *are hearing* outside of the family.

Correct: Children's reproduction of *their* parents' speech is deflected by the speech varieties they *hear* outside the family.

All these old Babylonian documents *are employing* the Babylonian script.

Correct: All these old Babylonian documents *employ* the Babylonian script.

4. I am teaching in America since forty years.

Correct: I've been teaching in America for forty years.

5. Oh, I am here already twenty years.

Correct: Oh, I've been here twenty years. (It is better to leave out the particle *already,* and to indicate its meaning by intonation and stress.)

6. I will do it, when I will come.

Correct: I'll do it when I come.

I can copy it for you, when I shall be in New York.

Correct: I can copy it for you when I am in New York.

7. I shall spend all my time in the pool, once I shall be up there.

Correct: I shall spend all my time in the pool, once I am up there.

8. I shall talk to him, whenever I shall have the opportunity. (This is correct, but wooden and pedantic.)

Correct and preferable: I'll talk to him whenever I have the opportunity.

9. I will report to you whenever anything should occur to me. (This sentence may possibly be defended but)

Correct and more idiomatic: I will report to you whenever anything occurs to me.

10. I have gone to the city yesterday.

Correct: I went to the city yesterday.

11. I have been born in the year 1895.

Correct: I was born in the year 1895.

12. I just received your letter. I just finished the book. (While these two sentences are probably frequently used by Americans in speaking and possibly also in writing, they are in the wrong tense for careful writers and speakers.)

Correct: I've just received your letter. I've just finished the book.

13. I didn't see him lately.

Correct: I haven't seen him lately.

14. He said, he will do, what he can for me.

Correct: He said he would do what he could for me.

I was told, that in the meantime the girls have fixed the date.
Correct: I was told that in the meantime the girls had fixed the date.

He asked me, what I think of that investigation.
Correct: He asked me what I thought of that investigation.

I thought, I am going to use the weekend for cleaning the apartment.
Correct: I thought I would (was going to) use the weekend for cleaning the apartment.

My father wrote, that the old gentleman may live for another ten years.
Correct: My father wrote that the old gentleman might live for another ten years.

15. I wish you would have told me about the meeting.
Correct: I wish you had told me about the meeting.

16. I am sure I had not found these men so willing to help without your recommendations (too literary and archaic).
Correct: I am sure I would not have found these men so willing to help without your recommendations.

WRONG WORD ORDER:

17. Here it is very cold. (This may, of course, be justified, but not as the usual translation of the relatively unemphatic "Hier ist es sehr kalt," but rather as a possible rendering of "H i e r ist es kalt"—gesperrt gedruckt.)
Correct: It's very cold here.

18. Interesting were the last lines of the long letter. (This inversion for emphasis sounds German. "Particularly interesting were the last lines of the long letter" would be possible, but)
Correct or preferable: The last lines of the long letter were particularly interesting (the adverb, *particularly,* giving the force of the emphatic German inversion).

19. I pay already too much attention to my colleagues.

Correct: I already pay too much attention to my colleagues (already should be dropped where possible).

20. We went all home.

Correct: We all went home.

It came all back to me.

Correct: It all came back to me.

21. I just would send you a wire to let you know the time.

Correct: I'd just send you a wire. . . .

22. I have not achieved yet much in the way of job hunting.

Correct: I have not yet achieved much in my job hunting.

23. My friend will drive me to Bridgeport and put me there on the train.

Correct: . . . and put me on the train there.

24. He brought me already two students to be tutored.

Correct: He has already brought me two students to be tutored.

25. Come right away home.

Correct: Come home right away.

26. The sun goes in the evening down at six o'clock.

Correct: The sun goes down in the evening at six o'clock.

27. He came very fast home in the car.

Correct: He came home very fast in the car.

FAULTY USE OF PREPOSITIONS:

28. The last song was composed from Schubert.

Correct: The last song was composed by Schubert.

29. I was in a party last night.

Correct: I was at a party last night.

30. He ran upstairs, hurried in the room and sat down out of breath.

Correct: . . . hurried into the room (hurried in the room would mean *hurried about* in the room).

31. I congratulate you to your birthday (to your success).
Correct: I congratulate you on your birthday (on your success).

32. He did not think on it (on it is biblical or archaic).
Correct: He did not think of it.

33. I felt so tired when I sat on your bridge table.
Correct: I felt so tired when (as) I sat at your bridge table.

34. I can have the apartment at the first of December.
Correct: I can have the apartment on the first of December.

35. With other words, this is what I want.
Correct: In other words, this is what I want.

36. With us in Germany, we did it differently.
Correct: We did it differently in Germany. (Be careful about using English translations of the German "Bei uns.")

MISCELLANEOUS MISTAKES IN GRAMMAR:

37. Now the Individualism has been overcome, but the Fascism remains a dangerous doctrine.
Correct: Now Individualism has been overcome, but Fascism remains a dangerous doctrine.

38. The father said, you must behave.
Correct: Father (or your father) said you must behave.

39. To make the long story short.
Correct: To make a long story short.

40. His hairs are gray. He has gray hairs.
Correct: His hair is gray. He has gray hair. (However, he has a few gray hairs.)

41. I like the idea of having someone here with whom I could be friend.
Correct: . . . with whom I could be friends.

42. You give not only technical advices on how to behave, but . . .
Correct: You give not only technical advice on how to behave, . . . (Advice has no plural in this sense.)

43. Are the news good?

 Correct: Is the news good?

44. There is the sun. She is trying hard to shine.

 Correct: There is the sun. It is trying hard to shine.

45. Raise the hand!

 Correct: Raise your hand (or hands).

 I did it with all the heart. They did it with all the heart.

 Correct: I did it with all my heart. They did it with all their hearts.

46. She looked at me with the eyes half closed and the arms hanging down like half drunk.

 Correct: She looked at me with her eyes half closed and her arms hanging down as though she were half drunk.

47. Come here and I'll put you on a dress.

 Correct: Come here and I'll dress you, or I'll put on your dress (or, I'll put your dress on).

48. I cut me in the finger.

 Correct: I cut my finger.

49. I am not too keen about the work, but *this* had to be a second consideration.

 Correct: *That* had to be a second consideration.

The use of *this* for *that* in sentences such as that above is widespread among Germans and should be watched, though it is hard to prove that it is wrong.

50. I report to her all what happened.

 Correct: I report to her all that happens.

51. I could let you know by Saturday in every case.

 Correct: I could let you know by Saturday in any case (or in any event).

52. Thanking you very much for everything you may do for me, I remain, . . .

 Correct: Thanking you very much for *anything* you may do for me, . . .

53. I flunked my test. I drove as badly as never before.

Correct: I flunked my test, driving as badly as I had ever driven (driving worse than I had ever driven before).

54. I saw him already once again (for Ich hab'ihn schon wieder einmal gesehen).

Correct: I saw him again. (The force of *schon* and *einmal* is expressed by the proper intonation and stress.)

55. It is lovely here, as usually.

Correct: It is lovely here as usual. ("It is lovely here, as it usually is," is also correct. Similarly, "He sang as well as usual" is said instead of "He sang as well as usually." "He sang as well as he usually does" is, of course, also correct.)

56. I came down by bus, since I don't have enough gas.

Correct or better: . . . since I haven't enough gas.

57. It is vacation and we have not to teach.

Correct: It's vacation and we don't have to teach.

58. I presume I have not to burden you with further recommendations (sounds a bit too literary and archaic).

Correct: I presume I don't (do not) have to burden you with further recommendations.

59. I am in the house as much as I can.

Correct: I'm in the house as much as I can be.

60. If your book gives many examples, it must become quite elaborate (possibly defensible, but it sounds more German than)

Correct: If your book gives many examples, it will surely become quite elaborate.

61. I like to tell you how much I enjoyed your lecture.

Correct: I should (would or I'd) like to tell you how much I enjoyed your lecture.

62. That should be a good book (as a translation of Das soll ein gutes Buch sein).

Correct: That's said to be a good book, or, they say that's a good book.

63. I would be very happy, if you were kind enough to see me (sounds archaic).

Better: I would be very happy, if you would be kind enough to see me.

64. I would not want that she tell that to everyone.

Correct: I wouldn't want her to tell that to everyone.

65. I don't like it, that she always acts so affectedly.

Correct or preferable: I don't like her always acting so affectedly.

Better: I don't like her affectation.

66. I don't mind that I do the extra work, but I do mind that he finds fault with me all the time.

Correct: I don't mind doing the extra work, but I do mind his finding fault with me all the time.

67. I should highly appreciate to make your personal acquaintance.

Correct: I should greatly appreciate making your personal acquaintance (or, meeting you personally).

68. That he is here, does not interest me at all.

Correct or preferable: His being here doesn't interest me at all.

That he always talks so loud, always gets on my nerves.

Correct: His loud talking always gets on my nerves.

69. I hope you will forgive me that I have not yet sent you the book you wanted.

Correct: I hope you will forgive me for not sending you the book you wanted.

70. He left without to say good-by.

Correct: He left without saying good-by.

71. May I visit you, when I should ever happen to pass through New York?

Correct: . . . if I should ever happen to pass through New York?

It will be your fault, when I get intolerably conceited.

Correct: . . . if I get (or should get) intolerably conceited.

72. He discussed with me what he would do, when he would be dropped.

Correct (if the meaning is conditional and not temporal): He discussed with me what he would do, if he were dropped (or possibly, if he should be dropped).

73. If I only think of it, I am getting mad.

Correct: I only have to think of it, to get angry (mad).

or, Whenever I think of it, I get angry.

or, The mere thought of it makes me angry.

MISCELLANEOUS MISTAKES IN WORDS:

74. He is a genial teacher. (Genial as a translation of the German *genial* is wrong. The English *genial* means lustig, heiter, leutselig.)

Correct: He is a brilliant teacher.

75. The included letter will introduce me.

Correct: The enclosed letter will introduce me.

76. We should look at it this way, isn't it?

Correct: We should look at it this way, shouldn't we?

You are happy in your present position, isn't it?

Correct: You are happy in your present position, aren't you? (Isn't it? as a translation for nicht wahr? or the French n'est-ce pas? is only possible in such sentences as, "It's cold, isn't it?" "It's wonderful, isn't it?")

77. I must make my hair.

Correct: I must do my hair.

78. I must make my preparations for my hours.

Correct: I must prepare for my classes.

79. I have come to a positive decision on your offer.

Correct: I have decided to accept your offer. (Positive does not mean affirmative; a positive decision means a definite decision and might even be a negative decision.)

80. I have great principle doubts about this chapter in this form.

Correct: I have great doubts on principle about this chapter in this form. (Principle as an adjective translation of the German prinzipielle is impossible.)

81. He remembered me to do it.

Correct: He reminded me to do it.

82. There is still a little rest of this influence in English.

Correct: There is still a little trace (or vestige) of this influence in English.

83. As said (as a translation of wie gesagt) sounds like a Germanism.

Correct: As I've already said.

84. And so goes life.

Correct: That's life, or, Such is life.

85. I had written a letter to Miss H. quite a while ago, as you had told me to do so.

Correct: As you had told me to (or, to do).

86. Would you kindly let me know soon that I can prepare the talk?

Correct: Would you kindly let me know soon, so that I can prepare the talk? (More colloquial)

87. If I want to go downstairs, so I can go down the back way also.

Correct: If I want to go downstairs, I can go down the back way also (or, then I can go down the back way also).

88. My speciality is art history.

Correct: My specialty is art history.

89. I was together with my girl friend all evening.

Correct: I was with my girl friend all evening. (Frequent use of *together with* in sentences like the above is surely a Germanism. *Together with* is possible in such a sentence as, "This experience, together with many others of a similar kind, convinces me that I was wrong.")

90. I have the firm intention to bring my English to a certain perfection during the next year. (This sentence needs to be improved in two places. "Ich habe die feste Absicht" can be

better rendered by "I am firmly resolved or determined," and "a certain degree" approximates the relative quality of "gewiss."

Correct: I am firmly resolved to bring my English to a certain degree of perfection during the next year.

91. I cannot fullheartedly encourage her.

Correct: I cannot wholeheartedly encourage her.

92. I hope I'll feel less lustless next week.

Correct: I hope I'll feel less listless next week.

93. We are, like usual, very busy.

Correct: We are, as usual, very busy.

94. The film was very good. (Not wrong, but not so often used as in German.)

Correct: The picture (movie) was very good.

95. I hope you received our German-written letters.

Correct: I hope you received our letters in German script.

96. My apparatus doesn't work.

Correct: My camera doesn't work.

97. Don't make such a scandal.

Correct: Don't make so much noise. (The English *scandal* means "oeffentliches Aergernis" only.)

98. I have so good cards.

Correct: I have such good cards.

99. There I'm skeptic.

Correct: I'm skeptical (about that). (Skeptic is rarely used as an adjective in English, and in the above sentence is a direct translation of Da bin ich skeptisch, and sounds like a Germanism.)

100. He winked at me with his handkerchief.

Correct: He waved at me with his handkerchief. (Americans and Englishmen can wink only with their eyes.)

SOCIAL FORMS
AND SOCIAL CUSTOMS
IN AMERICA

The books on etiquette and social customs in America, of which there are numerous excellent ones, fail to answer many of the questions on social conventions which Germans ask in America. For this reason there are included in this book five brief chapters on this subject, which, while containing much of the material in the standard books of etiquette, add additional new material and place it all in relation or contrast to German social forms, thus giving it the necessary stress and perspective. Though many of these chapters contain familiar information for older immigrants, it is hoped that the more recent immigrants may find them helpful. Those who desire further information are referred to the books of Emily Post and of others.

CHAPTER XXV

Greetings and
Other Social Forms

"HOW do you do?" is normally a greeting, not a question. The response to it is, "How do you do." It may, however, become both a greeting and a question, if it is repeated or receives special emphasis, in which case the response is, "Very well, thank you," or the less formal, "Fine, thank you." "How do you do?" quickly followed by "How are you?" is very frequently used. "How are you" is also a greeting, though a less formal one, which may become a question, when spoken with special emphasis or repeated. The response is, "Fine, thank you," or the more dignified "Very well, thank you."

After the initial greetings have been exchanged, the following expressions may be used: "I'm glad to see you," "I'm so glad to see you," and "I'm delighted to see you," the last two being more frequently used by women than by men.

"Good morning," "Good evening," and "Good night" are used just as their German equivalents. "Good day" is not used as a greeting at all, but gentlemen of the old school sometimes use it for leave-taking. "Good-by" is the most common form for leave-taking, though it is sometimes replaced, in very formal relationships, by "Good day" "Good afternoon," etc. "Bye-bye," though a favorite among the younger generation, is not yet acceptable to most of the older generation.

The greeting "Hello," though used by many educated American adults only among close friends and in informal relationships, appears to be replacing all other greetings, particularly among the younger generation, which uses it on all occasions and to all ac-

quaintances, whether close friends or merely "bowing acquaintances."

"I beg your pardon," "Pardon me," "Excuse me, please," and
"Excuse me" are the translations for "Entschuldigen Sie mich
bitte," and "Entschuldigung." In many parts of the country and
in many circles, these forms are being replaced by the English "I'm
sorry" and "Sorry," when an apology is in order, NOT, however, as
in the case of the others, to attract attention when requesting information. The response to these forms of apology is "Certainly,"
"Not at all," or "That's all right."

"All right" is also the indispensable translation, not only for
"Gut" and "Schon gut," but sometimes for "Ja." "Very well,"
which once was more dignified and polite than "All right," seems
to be losing ground, probably because it suggests to some an inferior relationship, e.g., of servant to master, private to officer, and
clerk to employer.

"O.K." as a substitute for "All right" enjoys wide use, particularly among the younger generation and in very informal relationships. It sounds, however, very incongruous, when it comes
from the lips of middle-aged or elderly German adults of professional groups. It is used correctly only when approving proof
(Druckproben) e.g., "O.K. with corrections" or when approving
reports to which one affixes one's signature, e.g., "I O.K.'d the report," for in these connections it has become fairly standard technical terminology.

There is no exact equivalent in America for "Auf Wiedersehen." "Au revoir" enjoys some currency and "Auf Wiedersehen" may in many circles be used with impunity. The slangy
"So long" expresses the same meaning, but is very informal, too
informal for general use. Moreover, it appears to be losing ground
rapidly to "I'll see you again," "See you again," or "See you later,"
and to the currently very popular but still somewhat slangy "I'll
be seeing you," which, when spoken cordially, comes close to
rendering the exact meaning of a heartfelt "Auf Wiedersehen."

"Yes, sir," "No, sir," and "Yes, ma'am," "No, ma'am," though often taught to children in school and at home, seem to be dropping out of favor, particularly with adults, who replace it by the plain "Yes" and "No" with a courteous inflection of the voice. "Sirring," that is, using "Sir" frequently, is, except in the Army and Navy, largely indulged in by boys from military schools and from "select" preparatory schools and colleges in the East and South. Servants are sometimes expected or required to use it.

"Yah" or "Yeah" as the equivalent of the German "Ja," though pronounced more slowly, is a very common substitute for "Yes" even among cultured Americans in informal relationships. Germans would, however, do well to use "Yes" in its stead.

SHAKING HANDS:

To Americans, Germans seem to be continually shaking hands. They shake hands when they meet and when they leave, on formal and informal occasions, apparently regardless of the degree of their friendship. They shake hands when they are introduced, when they receive a gift, when they are congratulated, "und dergleichen mehr."

It is difficult to generalize on American handshaking. One generalization is true, however, and that is that Americans shake hands much less frequently than Germans do. Some Americans shake hands fairly often, others do not. When men are introduced to each other, they usually shake hands. But when a man is introduced to a woman, the woman may or may not extend her hand. When paying social calls, some Americans shake hands, others do not, and no conclusions can be drawn from the shaking of hands or the absence of it. Salesmen and business men generally and politicians revel in the practice. Hosts and hostesses, as a rule, shake hands with their guests as they arrive and as they leave. American women do not usually shake hands when they are introduced or when they meet otherwise. The only advice that can be given to a German is to hold his hand in readiness; if he extends it too far he may have an embarrassing moment when his hand and arm dangle helplessly in mid-air.

INTRODUCTIONS AND LEAVE-TAKING:

Books on etiquette usually give the following fixed rules for introductions.

A man is always introduced to a woman, a younger person to an older one, a person to a group, and a guest to the hostess or host. When two men or two women are of the same age, it makes no difference which is introduced to the other.

The absence in these rules of any rule for introducing persons of inferior official, political, or social status to persons of higher status is significant. To make social distinctions in introductions is not the democratic American way. To differentiate between persons of various official rank may be a thoughtful courtesy to the higher ranked persons, but unless there is a great difference in position, the higher ranked person will not notice the order of introduction. Nor will slightly older people, if introduced to slightly younger people, think anything of it. The chief purpose of introductions is to get the preliminaries over with, and if the four rules mentioned above are observed, the conventions are intact. The exception to this rule is that women are always introduced to very high dignitaries of state or church, and sometimes also to guests of honor.

There are several correct ways of making introductions. One may say, "Mrs. Jones, may I present Mr. Smith?" or "Mrs. Jones, I should like to introduce Mr. Smith," or "Mrs. Jones, do you know Mr. Smith?" or even "Mrs. Jones, Mr. Smith."

In some parts of the country, among business groups or in athletic clubs, one frequently hears, "Jones meet Smith," or "Jones, shake hands with Smith." This variant is hardly formal enough to be cultivated by Germans; however, they need not be particularly shocked if they are so introduced.

The reply to any form of introduction that is always correct is, "How do you do?" Some people add the name as in "How do you do? Mrs. Jones," but the first form is sufficiently courteous.

The answer, "I am very glad (pleased) to meet you," is far less common than the German "Es freut mich," and while certainly not incorrect, might well be reserved for special occasions, as "I have heard so much about you, I am very (so) glad to meet you" (the sentences may be reversed), or "I am so glad to meet you, I have wanted to meet you for such a long time" (the order may be reversed).

When leaving someone after being introduced, one may say simply, "Good-by, Mr. Smith," or "Good-by, Mr. Smith. I am very glad to have met you," or "Good-by, Mrs. Smith, I hope I shall see you soon again (again soon)." The answer to this is "Thank you, I hope so too," or "Good-by, thank you." There is no perfectly acceptable translation for "Danke schön, gleichfalls." "The same here" is not good form.

When leaving the host or hostess after a party or dinner, the American may use any number of expressions, such as "Many thanks, we had a lovely evening (a lovely time)," or "I can't tell you how much we enjoyed ourselves," or "We had a fine (wonderful) time," "We've had such a good time," preceded by "Thank you."

"Schönen Gruss an die Frau Gemahlin (den Herrn Gemahl), Ihre Frau, die Eltern," usw., which many Germans regularly add to their good-bys, are rendered in English by "Remember me (please) to your wife, husband, family," etc., but they are much less often used. "My regards to your wife," etc. is less formal, while "Give him my best" is very, very informal.

Germans in America frequently comment on the importance many Americans attach to hearing and learning correctly the names of the persons introduced, it being not uncommon to say, "I'm sorry, I don't believe I understood your name. How do you spell it?" The need for knowing names is obviously more important at parties or receptions in America than in Germany.

where "Gnädige Frau" and "Gnädiges Fräulein" amply take care of all the women, and "Herr Dr." covers many of the men and will not be objected to by the plain Misters.

Contrary to the practice in Germany, it is the woman and not the man who has the privilege of acknowledging acquaintanceship by giving the first sign of recognition the next time or times the two meet after being introduced. If after several meetings the man can properly assume that the woman is likely to bow, he need not wait for her to give the sign of recognition, but may greet her first, or simultaneously.

CHAPTER XXVI

Manners and Customs in Public Places and in Homes

SHOWING deference to women or to older people and those in higher positions by giving them the position at one's right is not the American way. When walking on the sidewalk, American men give to women the position away from the curb; they may also give this position to elderly men, but among themselves there is no preferred position. When going through a door American men give precedence to women, to older people and those in higher positions, though the insistence on position by men is less important than in Germany.

American men are required by good form to take their hats off only to women and to girls beyond the adolescent stage. That means that they also take off their hats when they meet a man acquaintance accompanied by a woman or a girl whom they do not know. They never take off their hats to men alone. They exchange their greetings with a slight nod of the head, a smile of recognition, with or without an accompanying gesture of the hand. They may, particularly to close acquaintances, use a very informal non-military kind of salute, which may or may not touch the hat. They never bow very low or click their heels audibly, usually maintaining a very leger attitude and posture.

American men are expected to rise when a woman enters the room and whenever a woman rises from her chair in a room (unless she protests insistently against it), to seat the woman in restaurants, in all gatherings and even in the home, and to give their own seats to women in crowded places and of course also to elderly men.

They are also expected to take off their hats in elevators, particularly in apartment house elevators. (This rule is not always observed in crowded business elevators.) Many otherwise well-mannered men, however, keep their seats in the crowded New York subways, giving them up only to elderly persons of both sexes or to obviously sick or incapacitated fellow-travelers.

"You're welcome" is the customary response to "Thank you," "Not at all" to the less frequently used "I'm much obliged to you." "Thank you" is more cordial than "Thanks," as is also "Many thanks."

When words are not understood, "I beg your pardon," often abbreviated to "Beg pardon," takes the place of the German "Wie bitte?" and "Bitte?"

When refusing food Germans need to learn to use "No, thank you" for the rather ambiguous "Danke," which if the inflection is not clearly heard may mean either *yes* or *no*. "Thank you" and "Yes, thank you" are the phrases for accepting food or drink.

The translation of "Bitte, bitte" is, "Please," "Oh don't," "Please don't," "Oh don't bother," "It's no trouble at all"—the choice of the exact equivalent depending upon the stress and tone of voice that is given to "Bitte, bitte."

IN RESTAURANTS AND HOTELS:

When entering a restaurant, a woman may precede her gentleman escort, particularly if there is a hostess or a head waiter available to arrange for the seating. If you are seated at a table with strangers, it is not necessary to bow formally to them. If you seat yourselves, it is customary to ask, "Are these chairs (seats) taken?" In small resort hotels, many Germans bow formally as they enter the dining room and as they pass other tables on the way to their own table, but Americans dispense with this formality. After a few days they may give a slight nod of recognition as they pass and then a spoken greeting. The stage at which guests speak to each other in small family resort hotels is not reached so quickly in America as in Germany; on the other hand it is reached far sooner than in England. In such hotels an attempt to strike up a conversation after a few days' stay will seldom meet with a rebuff, as it might in England, and Germans may take the initiative without feeling that they are taking too much liberty or presuming too much.

TABLE MANNERS:

For some unaccountable reason, Americans, whether of British or continental European background, have developed a manner of eating which differs from that of their forebears. Whereas the cultured European manipulates the knife in his right hand and the fork in his left, raising the food to his mouth with the left, the cultured American starts out with the knife in his right hand and the fork in his left, only to place the knife on his plate as soon as he has cut a particular morsel of food. He then transfers the fork to his right hand and brings the food to his mouth with his fork in this hand. American writers on etiquette inveigh against this senseless procedure, but so far with little success, and this difference in customs usually sets Americans apart from Europeans. Since this process of eating is very inefficient, the American will usually cut whatever food is cuttable with his fork in his right hand in order to reduce the number of motions. Such strange methods naturally slow down the speed of eating, and Europeans will frequently find that they have finished with the food on their plates before their American companions, thus giving the impression of being fast eaters. Americans slow down their tempo of eating still further, when they eat (or drink) soup. They first move the soup spoon away from themselves to the far end of the plate before bringing the soup to their lips, and when they want the last drops they tilt the plate away from (and not toward) themselves. They also use the side of the soup spoon and not the tip.

OTHER DIFFERENCES:

Americans cut salad with their forks. Asparagus stalks and sweet corn on the cob are eaten with the fingers.

Germans are taught in their Kinderstube to place their hands on the table when they are not used for eating. Americans are taught to place them under the table.

SEATING ARRANGEMENTS AT TABLE:

The host sits at the head of the table with the hostess opposite him. If the custom of "bunte Reihe" does not work out with this arrangement, the hostess must change her position. As in Europe, the honored woman guest is seated at the right of the host, the honored man guest at the right of the hostess.

CHAPTER XXVII

Social Calls and Invitations

IN GERMANY the time-honored though now gradually disappearing ritual is for the newcomer in the community to make the first call, and the rules of etiquette require that the call be made on Sunday morning between eleven and one, with the callers in their Sunday best clothes (the man wearing his "Zylinder"), and that it last about ten minutes. The ritual for calling is quite different in America. Under no circumstances should the newcomer call first, unless invited to do so. That rule is now virtually the only fixed one remaining from more formal periods in American social life. In small communities and in certain cities, where the social life has remained formal, it is the older, established residents of the community who will call on the newcomers, probably in the late afternoon or early evening on any day of the week, but never between the hours of eleven and one on Sunday. This call may either be returned within a very short time, or the newcomers may invite the first callers to tea. In many communities it is considered acceptable form to invite the newcomers to tea or to some other social function without having gone through the formality of making a first call.

CALLING CARDS:

It used to be mandatory to deposit calling cards on a conveniently located little silver tray expressly designed for them, but this practice is now observed only in very formal communities. Every German should, however, have calling cards made, and good form requires that they be engraved, and that they contain nothing but the name, or names (except possibly the street address). IT IS THE HEIGHT OF BAD FORM TO HAVE TITLES APPEAR ON THE CARD. The accepted forms are as follows:

Mr. Karl Schmidt
or Mr. and Mrs. Karl Schmidt

Sixty-three Park Avenue

BUSINESS CARDS:

If business cards are used, they may carry additional information, but must OMIT such titles as Ph.D., Dr. Jur., etc.

LETTER HEADS—STATIONERY:

Titles must also be omitted from stationery, whether for social or professional purposes, except by Doctors of Medicine or Dentistry. The name, address, and telephone number may be printed on such stationery.

TITLES ARE RARELY USED IN AMERICA:

It is very important that Germans learn to forget about their titles in America except for very official purposes. As stated above, Doctors of Medicine or of Dentistry (and veterinarians) are always given their titles. Ministers who have received the honorary degree of Doctor of Divinity are frequently called Doctor, but Doctors of Philosophy or Science or Law are addressed as Mister (or Mrs. or Miss as the case may be) quite as often as they are addressed as Doctor.

In most of the older colleges and larger universities, professors and doctors on the faculty address each other as plain Mister or Mrs. or Miss and are often so addressed by their students. Even college presidents and deans may in many colleges be called Mister, except on official business or in official communications. In writing letters of recommendation for colleagues or students, a professor may, for the necessary purpose of identification, add his college position in parentheses below his name, e.g. (Professor of History), but in no case will he add his degree. Germans or

Americans, who in American colleges and communities try to insist on being given their proper and hard earned titles, or who use them without great discrimination, are usually the objects of indulgent smiles from their colleagues and their students. The custom in this matter varies from college to college and from community to community, but the trend is all toward the practice stated above, and Germans, with their long tradition of using titles, should be continually on guard, lest they innocently give offense.

ANSWERING INVITATIONS:

The rule for answering invitations is very simple. Formal invitations are answered formally, informal invitations informally. Thus,

Formal invitation (either engraved or written by hand):
    Mr. and Mrs. George Jones
        request the pleasure of
    Mr. and Mrs. Karl Schmidt's
        company at dinner
    on Friday, May the nineteenth
        at eight o'clock

Formal acceptance (written, never typed):
    Mr. and Mrs. Karl Schmidt
        accept with pleasure
    Mr. and Mrs. George Jones'
        kind invitation
    for Friday, May the nineteenth
        at eight o'clock

Formal regret (written, never typed):
    Mr. and Mrs. Karl Schmidt
        greatly regret
    that a previous engagement
        prevents their accepting

Mr. and Mrs. George Jones'
   kind invitation
for Friday, May the nineteenth
   at eight o'clock

When the invitation is informal and written in the first person, the reply is also informal and written in the first person. Thus,

Dear Mrs. Schmidt:
   I hope very much that you and Mr. Schmidt can dine with us on Monday, the fifth of January, at eight o'clock.

Sincerely yours,
Emily Fay

Informal answer:

Dear Mrs. Fay:
   We shall be very happy to dine with you on Monday, the fifth of January, at eight o'clock. Thank you so much for asking us.

Sincerely yours,
Maria Schmidt

Informal invitations on visiting cards may be answered informally on visiting cards, but using note paper for the answer is preferable. The hostess writes the invitation on the lower left hand corner of her calling card:

Friday
December fifth
Tea at four o'clock

The recipient of this invitation uses her calling card, writing:

Delighted to come, Friday the fifth.

or, if prevented from accepting:

So sorry,[1] cannot come, December the fifth. Will be out of town.

Formal invitations must always be answered. Informal invitations on calling cards often request an answer with the abbreviations R.S.V.P. (*Répondez, s'il vous plaît*).

---

[1] Note the "So sorry" in declining an invitation, but "sorry" as a translation of "Entschuldigung."

CHAPTER XXVIII

Letter Writing

AMERICAN letter writing is less formal than German letter writing and the rules to be observed are very simple to learn and to follow. It is thus possible, for example, to use "Dear Mr. ——" and "Sincerely yours" in all letters, without committing a faux pas, except of course when writing to high government or other officials. The usual rules are as follows.

"My dear Sir" and "My dear Madam" are the most formal forms of address. "Dear Sir" and "Dear Madam" are less formal. (In England, "My dear Sir" shows greater intimacy than "Dear Sir.") "My dear Mr. Smith" is more formal than "Dear Mr. Smith." Many Americans, however, seldom use the formal "My dear Sir," or "My dear Mr. Smith."

Begin the body of your letter after "Dear Sir" with a capital letter. If you use a small letter you may be accused of illiteracy.

The usual ending in business letters, "Yours truly" or "Yours very truly," is accepted practice with no perceptible difference in meaning. For all personal letters, "Sincerely yours" or "Very sincerely yours" are the conventional endings, again with no difference in meaning. To people very high up in authority and in submitting reports to august formal bodies, "Respectfully yours" is often used.

Avoid the use of "Dear Friend" as a translation for the German "Lieber Freund." If a German has reached the stage in friendship which would prompt him to say "Lieber Freund," all he can do in America to show that feeling is to write "Dear Jones" or "Dear Frank." "Dear Friend" is used in America largely by uncultured groups.

In writing business letters it is well to follow modern business procedure by avoiding formal business phrases and by cultivating an informal and even somewhat personal tone. It is now considered old fashioned and bad form to write: "We have your esteemed letter of the 15th instant and in reply beg to state"—or "beg to advise." In its place has come, "We have your letter of the 15th of April and desire (wish) to inform you," or similar variants.

A married woman receives the first name of her husband. Thus, Frau Maria Schmidt becomes Mrs. Karl Schmidt, socially and sometimes in business. Her signature is, however, Maria Schmidt, but in a business letter she may add below, in parentheses (Mrs. Karl Schmidt). On the envelope the only permissible form is Mrs. Karl Schmidt, never Mrs. Maria Schmidt.[1] Thus,

> Mrs. Karl Schmidt
> 20 Broadway
> Albany
> N.Y.

German women who find this apparent change of their sex amusing or absurd may be reminded of the equally absurd practice in Germany of giving women the title of their husbands, as in Frau Professor, Frau Ministerialrat, Frau Oberpostdirektor.

For men to sign their names at the bottom of letters without the first name, e.g., "Schmidt," is bad form. "Karl Schmidt" is the accepted form.

Although there are standard abbreviations for every state in the Union, it may be advisable for Germans, when addressing letters by hand, to write out the state in full to avoid the delay or loss in delivery which frequently may result from the failure of postal employees to decipher, e.g., the difference between N.Y. and N.J., not to mention other possibilities of confusion.

Germans should also learn to write 1 for *1*, and 7 for *7*, or letters may go astray.

---

[1] If, however, Mrs. Schmidt is in business or in a profession, she will often want to be known as Mrs. Maria Schmidt, or by her full maiden name.

The German manner of indicating the state in parentheses thus,

Hoferstrasse 110
Siegmar (Sa.)
Deutschland

is not used in America.

COMPLIMENTARY CLOSE:

Americans no longer make use of the obsequious complimentary close which was in fashion in Washington's time. Such expressions, therefore, as "Honored to be your most obedient servant" and "You may rest assured, dear Sir, of my sincere gratitude," are now utterly impossible in American letter writing.

Quite obviously the type of complimentary close will depend upon the nature of the letters, but in most cases nothing more need be said than,

1. "Thanking you for the interest you have taken in me"
2. "Thanking you in anticipation of your reply"
3. "Thanking you for whatever you may be able to do for me"

The following actual examples of the complimentary close in letters of Germans or Austrians are not good American form.

1. "In case you could find your way of recommending either of us by any chance you may be assured, dear Sir, of our sincere gratitude!"
2. "Thanking you in advance for your interest in the matter, I have the honor to be Your most obedient Servant . . ."
3. "Hoping not to meet with a refusal, and assuring you that I will do my best to merit your confidence and your protection in all respects, I am . . ."
4. "Please accept my application in a benevolent mood. With the expressions of my sincere gratitude I have the honor to be . . ."

CHAPTER XXIX

Tipping and
Bringing Flowers

THE rules for tipping are much less fixed in America than in Germany, where a 10 per cent tip is established practice, except where there is an "Aufschlag." In large cities in most parts of the country, tips are expected from the same quarters as in Germany. For small amounts in a restaurant the tip is likely always to exceed 10 per cent. Many Americans in large cities never tip less than ten cents even when the bill is under fifty cents, though doubtless tips of five cents are common enough for small bills. For bills of fifty cents and over up to eighty-five and ninety cents, it is customary to tip ten cents. If the bill is eighty-five cents, many Americans hand out a dollar with the words, "Keep the change." Tips are expected by taxi drivers, usually a ten-cent tip for small journeys, and correspondingly more for longer trips; by bootblacks and by barbers. Many American business men never tip less than twenty-five cents for a haircut, others feel that fifteen cents is sufficient for a fifty- or sixty-cent haircut. Hair dressers expect tips ranging from a dollar for expensive permanents down to smaller amounts for less expensive treatments. The tipping tariff for porters is regulated in some stations, at ten cents per item, but it is frequently added to. The porter in a Pullman car receives a minimum of twenty-five cents a day and fifty cents a night for his services. As in other countries the amount of the tip is naturally increased, if additional services are rendered.

Tipping domestic servants. It is not customary in America to tip domestic servants who help you on with your coat when you are leaving a private house. However, if you stay overnight, or for several days, it is customary to tip the servant or servants, or to give them a gift of some sort.

Since there is much less standardization in all these practices in America than in Germany, it is well to ask your friends in the communities in which you live what the prevailing practices are, thus avoiding either tipping too much or too little.

Bringing Flowers to Your Hostess:

Bringing flowers to your hostess when you are invited for dinner is a delightful German custom which will please American hostesses, but it is not an established practice and may be dispensed with, or at least not indulged in regularly.

DIFFERENCES IN
NATIONAL CHARACTERISTICS
AND TEMPERAMENT

CHAPTER XXX

The Problem of National Characteristics and Temperament

THAT there are differences in the national characteristics of Germans and Americans is apparent to all, and yet anyone who attempts to formulate these differences is certain to lay himself open to attack from both Germans and Americans—from Germans, because every German, from whatever part of Germany or Austria he may come, is convinced of the uniqueness of his regional characteristics; but also from Americans, who find it no less hazardous to ascribe common American characteristics to such diverse regional groupings as the New Englanders, the Southerners, and the Middle Westerners. When to these regional differences in both countries, other differences that are due to various political, religious, cultural, and occupational backgrounds are added, generalizations become increasingly difficult and vulnerable. And yet broad generalizations must be attempted, even at the risk of numerous exceptions. Germans who find some of these generalizations inapplicable to themselves will ignore them, and the conclusions drawn from them.

In setting down differences in national temperament and national characteristics generally, I have tried to avoid "Werturteile," judgments of value. If an admonitory tone has occasionally crept in, it is only because I believe that an adherence to certain German characteristics may often result in misunderstandings and complications, and that therefore adjustment to American characteristics may be indicated for those Germans who seriously desire "sich einzuleben in Amerika."

It would be a fascinating task to relate these differing national characteristics to the historical experiences that shaped them, but such a study would exceed the limits set for this book and besides might better be reserved to the trained historian or sociological-anthropologist, which I am not.

In the spirit of the foregoing paragraphs and with the convenient reservation that "all generalizations are false," I submit to German Americans the following generalizations on national characteristics, which are the outgrowth of many years of intimate association with them, that began in my boyhood in the Carl Schurz town, Watertown, Wisconsin, and have continued uninterruptedly and pleasantly through my studies and travels, my professional and social contacts up to the present day.

CHAPTER XXXI

Take It Easy

THE expressions "take it easy," "keep your shirt on," "hold your horses," "forget it," "skip it," "let it go," "what's the use?" are a clue to the American temperament. Their frequent use is less an evidence of excitability on the part of Americans than it is of their desire to avoid mental and physical irritation and the strain that follows it. The fact that there are no satisfactory translations for many of these expressions "lässt tief blicken." For example, neither "Mach' dir's leicht," nor "Streng dich nicht an," nor "Regen Sie sich nur nicht auf" render *Take it easy* adequately, for "Take it easy" covers both mental and physical attitudes.

The behavior of American crowds before box offices and elsewhere, and their natural forming into lines has been the subject of favorable comment from German observers, from the great historian Lamprecht down to the German journalist who spends a month in America and then writes a book on his impressions. Don't push, don't shove, don't get excited over trivial matters that can't be remedied—all express instinctive American reactions. "Temperamentvolle" foreigners should heed these admonitions in America.

NOTE: The following personal experience strikes me as applicable at this point. I had just returned from a sabbatical year spent in Germany, and was therefore particularly sensitive to differences between Germans and Americans. I had taken the 5.40 commuters' train to Bronxville (New York), which was due to arrive at 6.07, in ample time therefore for dinner at home or social engagements that began at seven. It was an express and Bronxville was the first stop. After crossing the Harlem River, the train came to a slow stop. Fifteen minutes passed. Nothing happened. A half hour passed and still the train did not move.

I looked up. All the other commuters, mostly men, were deeply immersed in the reading of their papers, apparently oblivious of everything else. The brakeman passed through the car. No one questioned him to find out the trouble. Forty-five minutes passed and still no motion of the train. The conductor came through the car. No one questioned him. Finally after a full hour, the train began to move, and eventually brought us home, too late for dinner and for social or other engagements. Surely this was an irritating and provoking experience, but one could never have gathered that from the behavior of the commuters.

I could not help comparing this experience with similar ones in Germany and on the Continent. Mere curiosity and a deep-felt sense of irritation would surely have prompted many Germans to say, "Was ist denn eigentlich los?" or "Das ist ja unerhört!" They would have struck up a conversation with their seat mates, giving vent to their feeling of injustice and frustration at this strange behavior of an otherwise very dependable railroad. They would have said, "Und das musste mir gerade heute passieren. Wir sind nämlich eingeladen," or "Mein Junge liegt schwer krank zuhause. Der Arzt kommt um halb sieben," und dgl. mehr.

But strange as it may seem, there was good sense to the behavior of these American commuters. There had been no collision. There was nothing they could do about it, even if they knew what the trouble was. The conductor, brakeman, engineer, and fireman would do all that could be done in the situation. So why worry about it? "Warum sich aufregen?" "Es hat keinen Zweck," "Man kann doch nichts machen." There was nothing to do but to *take it easy,* to grin and bear it, but these Bronxvillians did not even grin, they continued to read their papers with complete absorption and a "dead-pan" expression on their faces.

CHAPTER XXXII

Speech Habits

Restraint in Use of Qualifying Adjectives and Adverbs:

AMERICANS, particularly American men, are given to understatement in their use of adjectives and adverbs. Whereas a German might use "riesig nett" and "das war riesig nett von Ihnen," or "Ich tat es furchtbar gern," "das hat er fabelhaft gemacht," "famos," "glänzend," an American, to express the same sense of satisfaction or pleasure, might use, "That was very good of you" (or nice of you) and "I did it very gladly," "fine," "splendid." In a friendly golf match, a player who wants to compliment his opponent on a particularly good shot will say "well played," "good shot," "not bad," "that won't hurt you," or "that'll help you." A similar shot in Germany might elicit from an admiring and generous opponent "fabelhaft," "grossartig," "wunderbar."

However, American women and American girls particularly, frequently use "simply wonderful," "simply marvelous," "simply swell." For the same degree of pleasure, American men will use "fine" or the very slangy but expressive "swell."

NOTE: Professor Karl Reuning of Swarthmore College has written a very scholarly book entitled *Joy and Freude,* a Comparative Study of the Linguistic Field of Pleasurable Emotions in English and German. Professor Reuning summarizes his results as follows: Compared with the German vocabulary of pleasurable emotions, the English vocabulary lacks intensity, and it may be safely assumed that this is due to differences in the two national characters.

Speech Intensity:

The physical characteristics of the German language, such as the explosive glottal catch, the full, rich vowels ö and ü in such words as "böse" and "wüst," the very breathful enunciation of

most German consonants, particularly of such powerful conso-
nantal combinations as "Kraft," "plötzlich," "schrecklich," "Sehn-
sucht," "wichtig," "Schmerz," "Schmerzensgewalt," all give to
German speech a great tonal power. When to this physical intensity of the language Germans add an emotional intensity, the
result is likely to be a loud speech. It is only natural for many
Germans to carry over into English, even into conversational English, their German speech habits, and thus to hear their voices
rising audibly above those of their American friends in social
gatherings or public dining rooms. Some reduction of tonal intensity is therefore indicated.

CHAPTER XXXIII

Personal Dignity of Germans and Americans

AMERICANS in general, except perhaps Southern gentlemen, have a much less highly developed sense of personal honor than Germans. They may respond in vigorous language to what they consider a personal affront, but they are not so likely to make a vital personal issue of it as are Germans, to whom a reflection on their personal honor may be, if not a cause for the now outworn duel, a very serious matter that will demand a complete severance of relations, if a formal retraction is not forthcoming.

Affronts to One's Honor, Ehrgefühl:

Among the many illustrations that might be cited of the difference in reactions of Germans and Americans to affronts to their honor, is the following episode. A German émigré professor was once sent a bill for hospital services which he had never enjoyed. The bill was accompanied by a strong letter demanding payment. It was obvious that a mistake in names had been made, but the professor, thoroughly aroused by this reflection on his character and financial integrity, wrote a vigorous letter of reply (which an American might also have done). But in this letter of reply he demanded that the creditor write him a formal letter of apology or retraction for this reflection on his honor. Since no publicity could possibly have been given to this mistake, for mistake it was, most Americans in that situation, after getting the matter off their chests (or even without doing that), would have let the matter rest. If these Americans had given the matter a second thought, they would probably have said, "Oh, what's the use. Let it go."

NOTE: The above anecdote is probably not characteristic of German business men or of other Germans with more worldly experience than the professor in this anecdote. However, the fact remains that educated Germans are normally far more sensitive than educated Americans to what they consider affronts to their personal dignity and personal honor. At least that is the common judgment of Americans who know both Germans and Americans intimately.

Krachmachen, Krachschlagen, Anschnauzen—"Blowing Up" and "Bawling Out":

Many Germans, and not only those who have been "Unteroffiziere," often feel the urgent necessity of "Krachmachen" over serious mistakes and even minor omissions on the part of others. They then register this "Krach" by strong words, orally or in letters, of protest or by an "Anschnauzen" of the guilty one, if they are in a position to do so. They feel better for having gotten the matter off their chests, and their "Krachschlagen" and "Anschnauzen" often achieve desirable effects. Transferring this urge to America may have quite different results. Many Americans do, of course, occasionally "blow up" and "bawl out," but they seldom feel the better for it, and their display of strong emotion or temper is often interpreted by their hearers as an evidence of lack of self-control or of a weakness of their case. And to "bawl out" an employee or a student or any inferior publicly is the height of bad form.

Differences in Attitude Toward Superiors and Inferiors, Employers and Employees:

Many Germans and Austrians, particularly those of the older generation, show too great deference to their superiors. By bowing too often and too low, by nodding assent too frequently, and by being too solicitous of the point of view of these superiors, they sometimes lay themselves open to the charge of servility and obsequiousness. While Americans are expected to show proper deference to those above them, their manner is likely to be much more straightforward, direct, and man to man. Conversely, Germans in authority are apt to make a greater show of their authority in dealing with their inferiors, to order and command, instead of to suggest and direct. Americans in inferior positions are likely to resent the *tone* of authority, the "you have to do this" attitude. Their co-operation on a job, an assignment, or an enterprise can normally be much better enlisted by a suggestive kind of authority. This holds for relations in the classroom, the office, the workshop, and the home. Whether it is true or not that Germans enjoy working and living under discipline from above, the average American simply does not. In adjusting to American conditions it is important for Germans to learn these "rules of the game." The children of German parents quickly "catch on" to this new situation and may provide their parents with many anxious moments, until the parents catch on.

This difference in attitudes is particularly noticeable in older American communities with old Anglo-American stock. In Vermont, for example, purchasing labor or services from a Vermont farmer or craftsman or ordinary laborer does not entitle the purchaser to give orders. The Vermonter will co-operate with the purchaser of his goods or services, but he won't respond to a tone of command or order. "Your temporary power to purchase my goods or services does not entitle you to order me around" is his unexpressed attitude. In highly regimented industrial organizations there is obviously greater discipline from above, but even in such organizations the American point of view is likely to differ from the German.

To Illustrate:

The American employer's "I'd like to have you finish that for me by tomorrow, if you can," is probably the equivalent of the German "Ich muss das unbedingt morgen haben," or "Machen

Sie das für morgen auf alle Fälle," and should be so interpreted by a German employee. The fact that around New York City the phrase, "He didn't say 'positively,'" passes as a joke on the employee seeking an "alibi" for neglect of a duty or an assignment is further evidence on this point, if such evidence is needed.

CHAPTER XXXIV

"How Are You?"—"Fine"
"Wie Geht's?"—"Nicht Besonders"

GERMANS in America often comment on the frequent use of the word "fine" as the answer to the question, "How are you?" Accustomed to a wide variety of answers to "Wie geht es Ihnen?" such as "Gut," "Ich kann nicht klagen," "Na-so-so," "Nicht besonders," "Nicht gut," "Eigentlich nicht gut," "Schlecht," they may well wonder whether Americans are always physically and psychically "auf dem Damm." Of course they aren't, for they are beset by the same difficulties to which humans are heir, as are the Germans. To say that these differing answers reflect a difference in Weltanschauung, viz., the eternal optimism of the Americans and the deep-rooted pessimism of the Germans, while true in part, is not the whole story. The almost unvarying response "fine" has become a formula that may as frequently conceal as reveal the truth.

Repressing and Sharing Deep Emotions:

This difference in response may be better explained by the deep-seated reluctance on the part of cultured and reserved Americans to share with casual acquaintances, or even with intimate friends, their troubles and their mishaps; and conversely, on the part of Germans, by their natural urge to share with others, often unrepressedly, their own misfortunes and those of their families. Every American knows men and women among his acquaintances who carry some horrible mental anguish about with them, a hopelessly crippled wife or child or some other cruel affliction to which they never give expression even to their most intimate friends, and which they bar these friends from inquiring about and discussing. Americans are much more likely to "verstummen in ihrer Qual" than are Germans, and even when they don't, they speak about their afflictions with an absence of emotion that may strike Germans as heartless, though it may be anything else but that. However bad suffering in silence may be psychically for Americans (and Britons), it is for many of them an ingrained attitude or the only dignified thing to do.

CHAPTER XXXV

Making Friends in America

THOUGH not so quick at making friends as the Germans are, Americans, even those on the Eastern seaboard, thaw out fairly soon and become friendly. In certain parts of the country, in the Middle West and Far West, for example, friendships often develop very quickly, at least up to a certain degree, and an informal tone in conversation is soon reached. Herr Schmidt may on very short acquaintance find himself addressed as Schmidt, and sooner than he has expected it, the second stage of Karl Schmidt will be reached, and then Karl—often there is a passing over of the intermediate stage. He need not be affronted by this show of familiarity. It does not, of course, mean that the Duz-Brüderschaft stage has been reached. There simply is no American form for showing that state of intimacy. Nor is there any fixed ritual for reaching these informal relations as there is in Germany, where it is up to the older person, or the one in the higher position, to take the initiative. Though it is normally, or should be normally, the older man or the one in the higher position who takes the initiative in these matters, it would seldom occur to an American to find out the exact age of a friend before venturing upon informal forms of address.[1]

While American men quickly use the family name Schmidt or Jones in greetings and when referring to them in their hearing, American women who know Schmidt or Jones would never think of saying Schmidt or Jones in their presence, but would address them, or speak of them in their presence, either as Mr. Schmidt

---

[1] These sentences do not apply to the post-monarchical generation in Germany, which reaches informality almost as quickly as American youth.

or Mr. Jones, or as Karl or George, depending on the degree of their friendship.

Informality or familiarity in address is not, however, the prerogative of certain geographical sections of the country. The speed with which it is reached depends quite as much on occupational and social groupings. Among the individuals and groups that move quickly in this direction are politicians, salesmen, members of business clubs, members of athletic and social organizations, Y.M.C.A. secretaries, social workers and ministers. Members of academic and professional groups lag far behind.

The American Habit of "Kidding":

Many Americans reach the "kidding" stage, that is, the stage in which they make humorously intended personal or semi-personal remarks and allusions in the presence, and at the expense of their acquaintances, far sooner than Germans do. Germans would do well not to look upon such remarks as seriously intended, and therefore not to take personal affront at them.

The Friendly American Misinterpreted:

Germans frequently mistake a friendly reception of themselves and their projects for genuine interest and hence meet with cruel disappointments. A German looking for a position or for help of some kind may be met with, "I'll see what I can do for you," or "I'll consider you for the position," which, if nothing more definite is added, such as "Call me up again in a few days," or "I'll let you know by next Monday," is likely to be merely an evidence of friendliness or sympathy. In North Germany, where people are much more forthright, such friendliness might be considered as very encouraging to the candidate or to his project.

Talking Shop (Fachsimpeln) and Serious Conversation:

Many educated Americans strike Germans as being perversely averse to talking on serious intellectual matters and to "talking shop," even when that "shop" concerns vitally important problems. This characteristic may be observed particularly in social gatherings where the conversation may be kept on the intellectually low level of the exchange of social amenities, social banter, and trivia of one kind or another, far longer than a serious and intellectually minded German has any taste for. But even when two Americans meet for the express purpose of talking shop, there is frequently a preliminary time-consuming exchange of social amenities, before proceeding to the real purpose at hand.

TALKING SHOP IN INTERVIEWS:

Many Germans, particularly those looking for positions, are puzzled by this procedure. They have looked forward to being interviewed about their "Fach" qualifications, and they sit on the edge of their chairs, all eagerness to be questioned on their achievements, to elaborate on them and on their claims to the positions, only to find most of the interview taken up with matters that seem to them wholly extraneous. But the prospective American employer, quite apart from his instinctive desire to observe the social amenities, has "method in his madness." He has presumably read and analyzed carefully the paper record of the candidate before him, his vita and the documenting material, all of which has given him the necessary information on the Fachmann before him. What he therefore wants to know is more about the human being behind the Fachmann, his range of interests, whether he is socially agile and adaptable, whether his mind is flexible, in other words, the temper of his mind and personality. He believes that he can find the clue to the personality before him better in the give-and-take of ordinary conversation than in the prepared answers of the Fachmann.

CHAPTER XXXVI

German Gründlichkeit

GERMAN efficiency, attention to details, accuracy, thorough- ness, and punctuality, in a word German Gründlichkeit, are among the obvious virtues which Germans bring to America, and there can be little doubt that many Americans are sorely in need of them and would profit by adopting them. But a word or two of caution here may not be out of place.

Many Americans are not so inefficient as they appear to be at first glance; they DO get things done and often very efficiently with- out the fuss and stir and almost military precision of the Ger- mans. Many a German, who has worked in comparable organiza- tions in both Germany and America and was at first appalled by what appeared to him to be the unhurried, nonchalant attitude of Americans on the job, soon learns that the smooth, frictionless, co-operative working together in an American organization may very well accomplish quite as much as the tense and intensive but often nerve-wracking drive of a German organization. (There is, of course, little to choose between the standards of efficiency and precision that obtain in the best and most highly organized in- dustrial organizations of both countries.) And though "typical German thoroughness" is usually a great compliment when ap- plied to Germans by Americans, it can sometimes be a term of censure when it is applied to those Germans who in their instinc- tive love of details and accuracy and punctuality lose perspective and "make mountains out of molehills."

A little moderation in these matters may be called for in Ger- mans in adjusting to America, but not too much, for though

Americans, for example, are on the whole less punctual than Germans, punctuality in America still remains a cardinal virtue and the lack of it in Germans (or Americans) may have serious consequences in the social and business worlds.

CHAPTER XXXVII

Avoidance of Controversial Tone and Controversy

Rechthaberei und Prinzipienreiterei

AMERICANS on the whole are less likely to be rechthaberisch and to ride principles than Germans. They frequently appear to be, and frequently are, less interested in WHO was right or WHAT was right in a given situation, right ethically and morally, than in getting on with the job in hand—if by a set of principles agreed upon, well and good—if not, by compromises that are arrived at by various methods and devices. Such behavior, which is common also to the British, is often described by Germans as hypocrisy. While the German is interested in finding the ethical justification for a certain act, the Englishman will ask, "Is it cricket?" or "Is it done?" and the American, though not always using these questions, reacts similarly.

One result of this is that Americans will frequently not join the issue, but rather avoid it, both in social gatherings and in public and professional discussion. When a clash of viewpoints develops in social gatherings, a skillful hostess or host is expected to divert the conversation to less controversial matters. Discussions in American professional groups are as a rule characterized by much less intensity in the stressing of one's point of view, and often by an avoidance of the real issue. The manner of debate is usually suave, even when vital issues are at stake. When a decision has been reached, both sides of the contesting groups are likely to accept it in good spirit, and to remain, outwardly at least, on the friendliest terms with each other.

An absence of emotion is also characteristic of Americans when they present their learned papers to professional groups, or when they read or speak their reports to committees or governing boards in business or other organizations. To speak with emotional intensity on the results of research would strike most Americans as injecting a subjective element, a personal bias into something that should be coldly scientific, impersonal, and objective. Such apparent emotional indifference strikes the German, who enjoys "ganz in einer Sache aufzugehen" (see Note on p. 148), as evidence, not so much of complete objectivity, as of an unbecoming lack of interest in an important matter. Whereas the German scholar likes to state the conclusions of his scholarly research forcefully and often dogmatically, the American scholar, even when he is convinced of their invulnerability, will often put them forth hesitantly, reservedly, and modestly, at times even equivocally.

The discussion that follows such reports or papers in America is much more likely to be introduced by "I found the paper very interesting, but . . . " or "I wonder whether the speaker has considered the following point," and "Doesn't the speaker also believe that . . ." than by an abrupt "Ich bin durchaus anderer Meinung," "Leider kann ich mit der Ansicht meines Vorredners nicht übereinstimmen," "Ich bin grundsätzlich anderer Meinung," "Ich muss die Ansicht als abwegig ablehnen," or "Die Ausführungen meines Vorredners beruhen auf einer blossen Annahme."

The tone of scientific or intellectual controversy in writing is also different. Though German scholars have long since outgrown the bitter, war-like tone that characterized a major "wissenschaftlicher Streit" a generation ago, they still frequently attack contrary opinions with an unsparing and devastating directness. Americans who feel inwardly called upon to register their dissent in writing usually do so much more amiably. They will often take the sting from their criticisms by first pointing out the virtues of the article they intend to attack, and then they will proceed to a calm analysis of its defects—an analysis which again is characterized by the posing of questions, expressions of doubt, or other indirections rather than by direct, head-on collisions.

This same difference holds for other fields as well, mutatis mutandis, in the written discussion of public matters, for example. Even in business life in America, beliefs, ideas, and opinions are usually expressed less emphatically than in Germany. At first glance American political life might appear to be an exception, but surely only at first glance. American politics is a chapter by itself. Once every four years American politicians whip themselves into a fervor of excitement, but that excitement is usually properly evaluated and discounted by their hearers. And the rapidity and graciousness with which the losing side normally accepts the verdict at the polls, "plays ball," and "plays the game" are distinctly American (and British) phenomena in public life.

NOTE: I should not want these paragraphs construed as a condemnation of one of the finest of German characteristics. The fidelity to an assigned task, the complete surrender to an idea, the almost religious devotion to scholarship or to the arts that is expressed in such sayings as, "Die Wissenschaft ist heilig," and "Echte Kunst ist Gottesdienst," contrasted with the apparent casualness and indifference of many Americans in such matters (though the casualness is often not real but assumed) exemplify a quality which, except when sometimes carried to extremes, and particularly in the world of social and political action, is wholly admirable. And it is certainly a quality which Germans should retain in America, though they might do well to impose some slight restraint on their expression of it.

CHAPTER XXXVIII

Length of Speeches
and Talks

MANY Germans in America are likely in their speeches, addresses, or talks, whether to learned or professional groups or to women's clubs, to talk too long. Accustomed to audiences in Germany, to which they may talk for an hour or an hour and a half, they are similarly long-winded in America, often with disastrous results. A former president of Yale University was once asked by a speaker whom he had invited to address Yale students in their chapel exercises how long he should speak. The president replied, "As long as you want to, but I warn you that no souls are saved at Yale after twenty minutes." Now, while twenty minutes is obviously too short a time for a speaker who has important things to say, and while the length of speeches and talks is subject to a variety of considerations, such as the nature of the subject, the type of audience, and the number of speakers on the program, it is a fair assumption that in America very few souls are saved after forty or fifty minutes, and none at all after an hour or an hour and a half. Americans simply do not have the "Sitzfleisch" of the Germans.

NOTE 1: This limitation on time demands a wholly different treatment of the subject to be presented, as the following personal experience will illustrate. I once attended an international congress on education in Germany, which was addressed by Germans, Englishmen, and Americans. The Germans with their German Gründlichkeit and their desire for scientific exactitude invariably took up the first half hour of their talks with a résumé of what had been said before on the subject, the genesis of the problem, and a "Präzisierung des Themas" so that there would be no doubt in the minds of the audience on the underlying presuppositions and principles, before coming to the subject matter itself—which they would then develop with logical intensity and complete thoroughness. The Americans, either because they knew that they could not, in the thirty or forty minutes they intended to speak, clear up all possible misconceptions and come to complete agreement with their audience on definitions and terminology, or because they were constitutionally inhibited from speaking longer then thirty or forty minutes, would, after a few preliminary remarks designed to clear up only the grossest kinds of possible misunderstandings, state their themes and develop them in an informal causerie type of talk. The reactions of both Germans and Americans to these two types of public addresses were unfortunate for both Germans and Americans, not to say tragic. The Germans, used to exhaustive analyses and presentations of set themes, charged the Americans with superficiality, which was frequently anything but the case, as an examination of the written works of the Americans would have revealed. The Americans found the German addresses too long and physically and mentally exhausting. These unfortunate reactions were heightened by the fact that the Germans, better linguists than the Americans, were better able to follow the English addresses, while many of the Americans, unable to understand spoken German readily, were soon lost in the closely reasoned, carefully organized German addresses, which in form, that is, in length of sentences and wealth of detail, were exactly that of a written learned essay, rather than that of a talk.

NOTE 2: When definite limits of time are assigned to papers or talks, at scholarly or other formal meetings, such as fifteen, twenty, or thirty minutes, these limits of time should be religiously observed. When Germans, for example, are allotted twenty minutes for their learned papers, and are given the warning that their time is up, the good effect of their learned papers may be completely ruined, if they insist on going beyond the allotted time, even if the chairman graciously allows them a few extra minutes. In exceeding their time, they have irritated not only the chairman, though he may not show it, but also most of their audience and thus committed an unpardonable offense.

CHAPTER XXXIX

Form and Content
Gehalt und Form

STUDENTS of the national characteristics of the Germans and Americans all comment on the difference in stress which Germans and Americans give to form and content. Whether it be Goethe's *Faust,* which in content, i.e., in ideas, is unmatched in any other literature, but which in form reveals many imperfections, or the turgid, involved prose of many profound German philosophers and novelists, or the expression of life on the lower, everyday planes of human activity, the German is praised for his great emphasis on content, on ideas, and condemned or excused for his underemphasis on form. The American on the other hand (more so the Frenchman), is praised for his desire to reach perfection of form and condemned or excused for his underemphasis on content. Put baldly and therefore unfairly, the German and the American are contrasted thus: The German stresses content to the neglect of form, the American stresses form to the neglect of content. Though there are very many exceptions to this in both Germany and America, the generalization is roughly true.

The pertinence of this broad generalization in the higher realms of the arts need not concern us here. But there are implications in it for everyday living in America that are very important. To put it negatively: Departures from the ordinary conventions of life in America, exhibitions of taste that differ from the norm (and are therefore bad taste or poor taste), and personal vagaries in behavior are usually much more likely to come in for strong censure in America than in Germany. The content-stressing German, though he may object to such departures from accepted form or practice, will often excuse and even praise the perpetrator of them by stressing the importance of his ideas, or his essential worth. Though nonconformity in the field of politics is sanctioned by tradition, and therefore tolerated, nonconformity in the realm of form and good taste and accepted social behavior may quickly "finish" (erledigen) an American or German, both socially and professionally.

There is then no rugged individualism in such matters in America. For example, in the harmless field of dress, there is a standardization of style and taste that operates not only in the clothing of women but also of men, and radical departures from it may stamp the individualist as "queer." It is a strange kind of regimentation that rests upon custom and public opinion, and conformity in such and other matters, though it should not be fundamentally important, is more or less expected and required of both natives and foreigners. The degree of this regimentation varies with the size of the community, with the small community sometimes imposing its small town mores with an almost relentless insistence. And many a foreigner conscious of this social pressure can only shake his head over the paradox of living in a politically free and democratic America and having to conform to rigid local mores.

CHAPTER XL

Decisions by Principles
or by Compromise

THE antithesis expressed by the caption above is, of course, an oversimplification of the case. What is meant is that Germans are normally more reluctant than Americans to compromise, and that Americans frequently resort to some sacrifice of abstract principles, if their retention makes decisions either very difficult to reach or results in serious personal, social, or political consequences. This differentiation between Germans and Americans has already been noted in the paragraphs under Avoidance of Controversy, on page 146, but because of its importance it deserves further treatment.

The spirit of compromise which is characteristic of American (and British) legislative bodies and political life may, depending on one's political philosophy, be considered either a pillar of strength of American civilization or its glaring structural weakness. The overwhelming American opinion is that the disposition to compromise makes in the long run for a rough kind of justice and safeguards democracy, even while it undoubtedly results in the passage of faulty legislation, such as imperfect tax and tariff bills and contradictory social laws.

It may often mean "muddling through" in matters that seem imperatively to call for the "big stick" of executive or dictatorial powers, or the surgeon's knife, but it placates minority groups, prevents violent disputes and revolutions, thus ensuring governmental stability. Because of all this Americans are agreed that it is worth the high price that is sometimes paid for it.

This same spirit of compromise permeates organized activity on

every plane of American life and may be witnessed in the give
and take of social and home life. Everywhere there is the disposition to avoid head-on collisions and to reach compromises before
bitter feelings are aroused or serious wounds are inflicted. The
methods and devices sometimes invoked in this spirit strike many
a German as "unsachlich," not to say flippant. For example, in
such a minor matter as where a choice of entertainment is being
warmly argued by two persons or two groups, someone is likely,
long before the argument becomes heated, to say, "Let's flip a
coin. Heads or tails. All right. You win, so it's *Arsenic and Old
Lace* and not *Götterdämmerung.*" The dispute is thus over, the
loser accepts the decision in good grace, as a "good sport," and
an "enjoyable evening is had by all."

APPENDIX

SYNOPSIS OF THE VERB *TO BUILD*

<small>ACTIVE VOICE—INDICATIVE MOOD:</small>

Present Tense:	He builds
	He is building
Past Tense:	He built
	He was building
Present Perfect Tense:	He has built
	He has been building
Past Perfect Tense:	He had built
	He had been building
Future Tense:	He will build
	He will be building
	He is going to build
Future Perfect Tense:	He will have built
	He will have been building

<small>PASSIVE VOICE:</small>

Present Tense:	It is built
	(Depending on the context this means either Es wird gebaut or Es ist gebaut)
	It is being built
Past Tense:	It was built
	(Es wurde gebaut or Es war gebaut)
	It was being built
Present Perfect Tense:	It has been built
Past Perfect Tense:	It had been built
Future Tense:	It will be built
	(It is going to be built)
Future Perfect Tense:	It will have been built

SUBJUNCTIVE MOOD—ACTIVE VOICE:

If he build it of stone, the cost would be excessive. ("If he build" is not frequent in conversation.)

If he built it of stone, the cost would be excessive ("built" same as indicative).

If he should build it of stone, the cost would be excessive.

If he would build it of stone, the cost would be excessive.

If he had built it of stone, the cost would have been excessive.

Had he built it of stone, the cost would have been excessive.

SUBJUNCTIVE MOOD—PASSIVE VOICE:

If it be built of stone, the cost would be increased. ("If it be built of stone the cost would be increased" is not frequent in conversation.)

If it were built of stone, the cost would be increased.

If it had been built of stone, the cost would have been increased.

SUBJUNCTIVE FORMS OF THE VERB TO BE:

If he be ready, it would be fine. ("If he be ready" is infrequent in conversation.)

If he were ready, he would come.

Were he ready he would come. (In conversation, the indicative "if he was ready" is often used.)

If he had been ready, he would have come.

Had he been ready, he would have come.

NOTE: See also chapters on *Shall* and *Will* and *Going,* and *Should* and *Would*.

PREPOSITIONS

Learning the correct use of prepositions constitutes one of the greatest difficulties in learning a language. The prepositions governed by verbs, nouns, and adjectives are particularly troublesome. For this reason a large list has been compiled of words and phrases that govern prepositions different from those that would be used in German. A few of the examples given are equivalent to cases in German without a preposition. While the list is by no means exhaustive, it does contain a large number of the common examples. It has been classified alphabetically under the various prepositions. Such an arrangement has the advantage of indicating the nature and scope of the most used prepositions; however, it hampers easy looking up. Germans who are not certain of the right use of the prepositions listed would do well to collate the whole list and arrange it alphabetically, thus facilitating easy reference.

ABOUT

annoyed about
anxious about
argue about (disputieren)
ask about (fragen nach)
bother about (sich kümmern um)
care about (sich kümmern um)
complain about (sich beschweren über)
get enthusiastic about (sich begeistern für)
have a dispute about
inquire about (from someone)
not another word about it (kein Wort mehr davon)
speak about (sprechen über)
upset about
worried about

AT

amused at
angry at (a thing—with a person)
arrive at
astonished at
astounded at, by
at a gulp (auf einen Zug)
at any (no) price
at dinner
at one blow
at play
at stake (auf dem Spiel)
at the bottom of it (steckt dahinter)
at the moment
at the next station
at what time
at work

At

at (on) your advice (auf deinen Rat)

at your disposal (zu Ihrer Verfuegung)

at your service

close at hand (bei der Hand)

discovered at (cheating)

disgusted at (a thing)

get at him (ihm bekommen)

good at (cards)

grumble at

hint at (auf etwas anspielen)

indignant at

laugh at

mock at (spotten über)

poor at (golf)

sell at a loss (profit)

smile at

surprise at

wonder at

work at

Between

between us (unter uns)

Beyond

beyond all doubt (über jeden Zweifel erhaben)

By

by all means (um jeden Preis)

by land

by no means (um keinen Preis)

by water

by your leave (mit Ihrer Erlaubnis)

day by day

profit by

set store by it (Wert darauf legen)

side by side (Seite an Seite)

stick by someone (jemandem zur Seite stehen) (stick to the point)

understand by (verstehen unter)

For

apply for (sich bewerben um)

ask for (bitten um)

call for (abholen)

concerned for (troubled)

cry for (weinen um)

desire for (Wunsch nach)

eager for

fight for

for example

for the first time

for this reason

give cause for (Grund geben zu)

hope for

hunger for

hunt for

long for (rest)

look out for someone (auf jemanden aufpassen)

reach for (darnach greifen)

search for

send for

strive for

thirst for

wait for (warten auf)

wish for (etwas wuenschen)

yearn for

From

different from (anders als)

from the bottom of my heart (aus tiefstem Herzen)

keep something from (etwas vor jemandem verheimlichen)

suffer from

In

abound in (reich sein an)
acquiesce in
bear in mind (an etwas denken)
believe in
concerned in (interested)
concur in (an opinion)
confide in (entrust a secret)
deal in (handeln mit)
decrease in
engage in
fail in one's examination (durchs
   Examen fallen)
faith in
in any case
in broad daylight (bei hellem
   Tage)
increase in (strength)
in German (auf deutsch)
in good humor (bei guter Laune)
in name only
in other words
in part (zum Teil)
interest in
in this manner (auf diese Weise)
in time (zur rechten Zeit) (mit
   der Zeit)
joy in
lacking in
lie in wait (auf der Lauer liegen)
persist in (auf etwas bestehen)
take part in
take pleasure in (Gefallen an
   etwas haben)
participate in
poor in (goods)
rich in (goods)
share in
wanting in

Of

admit of (permit) (etwas zulas-
   sen)
afraid of (sich fürchten vor)
ashamed of
be considerate of (Rücksicht nehmen auf)
beware of (sich hüten vor)
boast of
capable of
careless of, about
complain of
composed of (bestehend aus)
consist of, in (bestehen aus)
cure of
die of
desirous of
envious of
fear of
forgetful of
glad of (an opportunity)
guilty of
hatred of (the enemy)
hopeful of (recovery)
horror of
inquire of (a person—about a
   thing or person)
innocent of
jealous of
judge of (urteilen über)
lack of
love of
made of
make much of us (viel auf uns
   halten)
makes fun of
memory of (Erinnerung an)
neglect of
of one's own accord (auf eigene
   Initiative)

OF

proud of
recollection of (Erinnerung an)
remind one of
reminiscent of
repent of
sensible of (his obligations)
smells of (cabbage)
suspicious of
take advantage of (sich etwas zu
  Nutze machen)
tastes of (garlic)
thoughtful of
tired of
treat of (behandeln)
weary of

ON

authority on (a subject)
confer upon, on (a Ph.D. degree)
congratulate on
decide upon, on (a plan)
depend on (ankommen auf)
dependent on, upon
determine upon, on
have views on
insist upon, on (auf etwas bestehen)
keen on (sehr darauf aus sein)
live on (leben von)
lost on him (an ihm verschwen-
  det)
on that day
on the contrary
on the grounds of (aus Gründen)
on the other hand
on the spot (an Ort und Stelle
  sein)
on the spur of the moment (aus
  dem Stegreif)

on the stock exchange (an der
  Börse)
on the whole (im ganzen)
on this occasion
on time
suffer on her account (um sie
  leiden)
take revenge on
wait on (servieren)

OUT

dine out (ausser dem Hause
  speisen)

TO

accustom to
adapt oneself to (sich anpassen an)
address oneself to (sich wenden
  an)
adhere to
agree to (eingehen auf)
all to myself (ganz für mich)
allude to
amount to (sich belaufen auf)
apply to someone (sich an jemanden wenden) That applies to
  (bezieht sich auf)
aspire to
attach to (befestigen)
attention to (auf etwas achten)
averse to
beneficial to
blind to
civil to
confess to
confine to
conform to
common to
cruel to
deaf to
decide to (sich entschliessen zu)

drink to (anstossen auf)
engaged to (verlobt mit)
essential to
faithful to
fasten to
fatal to
favorable to
good-by to
hold a person to his promise (je-
    mandem beim Wort nehmen)
in answer to
indifferent to
indispensable to
inferior to
in regard to
in reply to
in respect to, of
just to
keep something to oneself (etwas
    für sich behalten)
keep to oneself (sich für sich hal-
    ten, allein bleiben)
kind to
lay claim to (Anspruch machen
    auf)
lends itself to (eignet sich)
limit to (beschränken auf)
look forward to with pleasure
    (sich freuen auf)
married to
near or near to (the city)
obedient to
object to (Anstoss nehmen)
partial to (eingenommen für)
pay a visit to
peculiar to
polite to
preparatory to
prior to
recommend to (empfehlen)

refers to (sich auf etwas beziehen)
resign oneself to (sich abfinden
    mit)
respond to
sensitive to (his faults)
stick to the point (bei der Sache
    bleiben) (stick by someone)
subscribe to, for
superior to
that is up to you (es steht bei dir)
tie to
to one's heart's content
with regard to
write to

Toward

friendly toward

Under

under one's very nose (jemandem
    vor der Nase)

Up

look something up (etwas nach-
    schlagen)

With

angry with (a person—at a thing)
deal with (behandeln)
disappointed with
disgusted with (a person)
find fault with (etwas aussetzen
    an)
indignant with (a person)
in love with (verliebt in)
part with (their rings, e.g., to sell
    them)
sick with
wet with
with all my heart

TRITE OR HACKNEYED PHRASES, CLICHÉS

Every author of a handbook of English lists a large number of phrases that have been worn thin through overuse, and guards students against their use. One author goes so far as to say that they are now used only for humor or irony, which is a gross exaggeration.

The use of such clichés for purposes of irony or satire is well illustrated by the following paragraph taken from one of the clever "Profiles" in *The New Yorker*, which characterizes a well-known military expert:

". . . The Major always, whether orally or in print, makes it crystal-clear that opportunities are golden, experience is bitter, flies are in the ointment, and, regardless of how famine may gnaw at the vitals, nobody can have his cake and eat it too without winding up in a grave dilemma."

Though many of those listed have been worn pretty thin, no user of English can dispense with them in everyday speech or even in formal writing. The careful writer will, of course, use them sparingly, but they are nevertheless part and parcel of everyone's work-a-day vocabulary and hence INDISPENSABLE to every foreigner learning English.

a bolt from the blue
abreast of the times
aching void
after all has been said
after all is said and done
agree to disagree
all in all
all work and no play
a long-felt want
ardent admirers
arms of Morpheus
as black as pitch
as luck would have it

as slippery as an eel
at a loss for words
at one fell swoop
bathed in tears
beat a hasty retreat
beggars description
better half
better late than never
bitter end
blissfully ignorant
blushing bride
brave as a lion
brawny arms

breathless silence
breathless suspense
briny deep
brown as a berry
budding genius
busy as a bee
by leaps and bounds
captains of industry
caught like rats in a trap
center of attraction
checkered career
cheered to the echo
clear as crystal (crystal clear)
clinging vine
close to nature
cold as ice
completes the picture
conspicuous by his absence
course of true love
Dame Fortune
deadly earnest
depths of despair
devouring element
discreet silence
doomed to disappointment
downy couch
drastic action
dull (sickening) thud
each and every
easier said than done
epic struggle
equal to the occasion
exception proves the rule
fair sex
familiar landmark
fast and furious
favor with a selection
festive occasion
few and far between
fiber of his being

filthy lucre
fools rush in
force of circumstances
goes without saying
great open spaces
green with envy
hands across the sea
he-man
holy bonds of matrimony
in all its glory
in great profusion
iron constitution
irony of fate
it stands to reason
justice to the occasion
last but not least
last straw
light fantastic
limped into port
lonely sentinel
mad as a wet hen
mantle of snow
meets the eye
method in his madness
monarch of all I survey
more in sorrow than in anger
Mother Earth
motley crowd
needs no introduction
nestles in the hills
nipped in the bud
none the worse for his experience
none the worse for wear
no sooner said than done
partake of refreshments
poor but honest
powers that be
presided at the piano
promising future
proud possessor

psychological moment
put in an appearance
reigns supreme
rendered a selection
replete with interest
riot of color
ripe old age
royal reception
ruling passion
sadder but wiser
sad to relate
sea of faces
seething masses of humanity
sigh of relief
silence reigned supreme
simple life
single blessedness
skeleton in the closet
sleep of the just
slow as molasses
slow but sure
soul of honor
struggle for existence

sturdy as an oak
sweat of his brows
table groaned
the plot thickens
the time of my life
tired but happy
too full for utterance
too funny for words
venture a suggestion
walk of life
watery grave
wee small hours
wends his way
where angels fear to tread
where ignorance is bliss
with bated breath
words fail to express
work like a Trojan
worse for wear
wrapped in mystery
wreathed in smiles
wrought havoc
wry countenance

THE SPELLING AND PRONUNCIATION
OF NAMES AND FOREIGN WORDS

Ever present pitfalls for Germans are the English spelling and English pronunciation of Proper Names, Biographical Names, Geographical and Foreign Names. In order to avoid mistakes, it would be well for Germans to assume that the spelling or the pronunciation (or both) of such names differ in Germany and America, and to consult an English dictionary in each case for the correct English spelling and pronunciation. The following few examples of names either differently spelled or pronounced, or both, should suffice to indicate the importance of this warning.

NAMES SPELLED THE SAME BUT PRONOUNCED DIFFERENTLY:

Niagara	Euridice
Hiawatha	Eureka
Cicero	Paris
Caesar	Amsterdam
Vergil	Rotterdam
Tacitus	Marseilles
Homer	Bethlehem
Odysseus	Canaan
Plato	Nazareth
Sophocles (k)	Babylon
Euripides	Babel

NAMES SPELLED DIFFERENTLY AND PRONOUNCED DIFFERENTLY:

Sicily	Sizilien
Naples	Neapel
Bruges	Brügge
The Hague	Der Haag
Turkey	Die Türkei
Nice	Nizza
Maecenas	Mäzen
Aristotle	Aristoteles

Charlemagne	Karl der Grosse
Matthew	Matthaeus
Brazil	Brasilien
Milan	Mailand
Liége	Lüttich
Geneva	Genf
Norway	Norwegen
Athens	Athen
Mercury	Merkur
Iliad	Ilias
Attila	Etzel
Horace	Horaz
Nile	Nil
Argentina	Argentinien

AMERICAN AND GERMAN
EDUCATION

Among the Germans who have immigrated to America since 1919 there are not only a large number of parents, but also many teachers and professors, many of whom find an understanding of American education and of American pupils and students no simple matter. A few observations on the differences between American and German education may therefore prove helpful.

It is relatively easy to generalize on German education. State-controlled as it is, there are fewer differences in the quality of university, secondary, and primary education in Germany than in America. German universities and schools have, in general, the same requirements, the same programs (the same pensum for each type of university and school) and are on the same level. In America there are still great differences in the quality of universities, colleges, and schools. While the best American universities and colleges, for example, are easily the equal of the best German institutions of higher learning, there are still many, particularly in the newer or less prosperous sections of the country, whose standards are below those of the German university. In addition, the American student body is less homogeneous than the German, due to the democratic conception of American education, which makes it possible for large numbers of economically and culturally underprivileged groups to take advantage of higher education, and also to the mixed heritages of the American student body.

Some of the resulting differences are as follows:

1. German teachers and parents will find American pupils and students, as compared with German, weak in the language studies. There are at least two reasons for this: (a) the foundations of grammar are less thoroughly taught, (b) apart, however, from the fact that German teachers usually demand greater accuracy in the fundamentals of grammar, sometimes even teaching grammar for grammar's or accuracy's sake, American students, most of whom live thousands of miles away from foreign-speaking people, think of the foreign language as something to be read and not spoken. They are therefore less aware of

the utilitarian, social, and cultural values of speaking the foreign language and of understanding it AURALLY. In addition, because of their mixed background, American students speak and write English less well, on the whole, than German students speak and write German.

2. Many American pupils and students reveal an abysmal ignorance of continental European history and geography. While the majority of American college students have had courses in European history, continental Europe is so remote to them that they quickly forget what they have learned.

3. European architecture, and the plastic arts generally, with which Germans have grown up, are often largely picture book matters to American youth, and even an elementary knowledge of various art forms cannot be taken for granted. Twenty years ago the same generalization would have held for the knowledge of classical music, but today the widespread listening to classical music on the radio and the tremendous sales of symphony records to American homes is rapidly raising the standard of musical knowledge and musical appreciation on the part of the American youth.

4. Having suffered less than German youth, both as individuals and as members of a nation, American youth is much less given to introversion, to introspection, to Weltschmerz, to pessimism, to philosophizing, and to abstract thinking than the comparable German youth in the same age groups.

Offsetting this, there are, however, several characteristics of American youth that are definitely on the asset side:

1. Not given to abstract thinking and to set philosophies of life, they often show a freshness of approach to intellectual problems, which is untrammeled by strong prejudices and dogmas. They are thus frequently able, by their very naïveté and by reflections of a more pragmatic sort and by common sense, to penetrate deeply into a problem and find the solutions for it, unhampered by the impediments of strong preconceptions and age-old heritages. This quality makes them amenable and responsive to good teaching. And because of their innate freshness of approach and outlook, their optimism, their immaturity (if you will), they are less likely to be defeated or overwhelmed by personal and world problems than the prematurely tired youth of older civilizations.

2. Their knowledge of British history is naturally greater than that of German youth, for British history is widely taught in American

schools and colleges, and British literature, both past and contemporary, is as much the heritage of American students as it is of British.

3. In the natural sciences and in all subjects requiring manual aptitude and manual dexterity, American youth is likely to be superior to the average German youth. Many American boys, even from well-to-do homes, have been "making things" and "fixing things" in the time that German boys in similar families were devoting to other pursuits. Moreover, American boys of middle-class families almost without exception are familiar with automobiles and many of them have played with cheap forty- and fifty-dollar jalopies which they have to repair continually or even take apart. They thus become machine- and mechanically minded and can transfer their acquired skills to the subjects which require manual dexterity. In addition, this practical experience gives to many of them a practical turn of mind which they carry over into their outlook on life. American girls, on the other hand, are less practical than German girls, who have had in German schools and homes a great deal of practical training.[1]

DIFFERENCES IN CLASSROOM ATTITUDES:

The attitude of American pupils and students toward their teachers and professors is different from that in Germany. The American boy or girl, young man or young woman, does not stand in awe of his teacher or instructor, as was often the case in monarchical and even in Republican Germany. American teachers obtain the best results in their subjects and in their discipline, not so much by the exercise of authoritarian power as by the persuasive nature and reasonableness of their demands on their students. The relationship between students and teachers in America is likely to be one of friendliness and comradeship. The superior American teacher is the one who succeeds in combining a personal interest in his students with high educational requirements. This friendly and personal atmosphere of the American classroom has, as one result, the development of a high degree of self-discipline on the part of the students, who far less often than in many other countries are likely to try to take advantage of their teachers by doing dishonest work (witness the successful operation in many schools and colleges of the

---

[1] I am comparing here American high school, college, and university students with German gymnasium and university students. The German youth that leaves school at the age of fourteen and enters upon a period of apprenticeship in German crafts is known to receive a far better mechanical training than a similar American youth.

so-called honor system, under which students take examinations without ANY supervision on the part of their teachers). This classroom discipline has its counterpart in American homes, where in the opinion of most cultured Americans better results are obtained by sympathetic understanding and friendly reasoning than by displays of parental authority.

NOTE: This brief, and therefore necessarily superficial, analysis of the differences between American and German education is included at the urgent request of a German-born colleague, who both as teacher and parent believes that a few paragraphs on this subject belong in this book.

SOURCES OF INFORMATION ON AMERICAN EDUCATION

The multiplicity of schools and colleges in America and their varying standards and practices are confusing to German parents. In this confusion they are not alone, for American parents find no easy answers to the questions they raise on the education of their children. The sources of information to which Germans in America should go for their answers are:

1. Informed American friends, particularly such friends as may be in the teaching profession.

2. Grade School advisers and Principals in High Schools.

3. The United States Office of Education, Department of the Interior, Washington, D.C. This federal agency publishes a large number of pamphlets and will answer all questions dealing with education in America. Its Foreign Division is well informed on the differences between American and European education.

4. The Institute of International Education, 2 West 45th Street, New York City, has qualified experts in the field of college education and is also informed on European education.

5. The following handbooks contain all available information on Junior Colleges, Colleges, and Universities, on courses of instruction, tuition and other costs, educational requirements and facilities:

American Junior Colleges, Published by the American Council on Education, Washington, D.C.

American Universities and Colleges, Published by the American Council on Education, Washington, D.C.

The College Blue Book, by Huber Hart.

CONTRIBUTIONS
OF THE GERMAN ELEMENT
TO THE UNITED STATES

Faust, A. B. *The German Element in the United States.* 3 volumes. Published in 1909 by Houghton Mifflin Company. Revised in 1927 and published by the Steuben Society. Though somewhat out of date, it is still indispensable.

Wittke, Carl. *We Who Built America: The Saga of the Immigrant.* Published in 1939 by Prentice-Hall. An interesting account of the contributions of various nationalities to the building of America.

Francke, Kuno. *The German Spirit.* Published by Henry Holt and Company, 1916.

Münsterberg, Hugo. *American Traits from the point of view of a German.* Published by Houghton Mifflin Company, 1901.

The Americans. 1905.

Aus Deutsch-Amerika. Berlin, 1909.

Kuno Francke and Hugo Münsterberg, both native Germans and both for many years professors at Harvard University, were prolific writers on German American problems and on the differences between Germans and Americans. The above books, as well as many other books and articles by them, are well worth reading.

Schurz, Carl. *Reminiscences of Carl Schurz.* 3 volumes. The fascinating autobiography of the greatest German American. Forty-eighter, friend of Lincoln, soldier-statesman, he synthesized the finest of German and American characteristics. Sponsored civil service reform.

The Carl Schurz Memorial Foundation, Philadelphia, Pa. Those who are interested in the contributions of the German element to the United States are referred to this Foundation, which is becoming the recognized depository for Americana-Germanica, and which publishes bi-monthly The American-German Review.

BIBLIOGRAPHY
ON THE AMERICAN WAY
Prepared and Annotated by Virginia Harrington

Assistant to the Dean and Assistant Professor of History at Barnard College

The most famous general survey of the history of the United States is undoubtedly Charles and Mary Beard, *The Rise of American Civilization* which appeared in 1927. *America in Midpassage* carries the story down to the outbreak of war in 1939–1940, and a recent volume, *The American Spirit,* attempts to answer the question, "What have representative—often great—Americans believed the intellectual and moral contributions of the United States to have been?" More of a textbook, but nevertheless exceedingly well done both in style and content, and equipped with excellent critical bibliographies, is Morison and Commager, *The Growth of the American Republic, 1000 to 1942,* 2 volumes.

Very little attention has been paid on the whole to the development of the American spirit or to answering the question first posed in the eighteenth century, "What makes an American?" Most such comment has come from foreign observers like Alexis de Tocqueville (*Democracy in America*) or Lord Bryce (*The American Commonwealth*). Recently, however, under pressure of political developments both at home and abroad, much has been written defining and defending "the American way of life." Many of these articles are, of course, simply campaign literature, but a scholarly and brilliant study which is extremely valuable for understanding this important phase of American thinking is Ralph Gabriel, *The Course of American Democratic Thought.* A small collection of documents and speeches which may be considered milestones in the development of American political thinking is Stuart Brown, *We Hold These Truths.* For the development of philosophy as such in America see Woodbridge Riley, *American Thought from Puritanism to Pragmatism and Beyond.*

The best general survey of American literature is V. L. Parrington, *Main Currents in American Thought,* a fascinating though occasionally somewhat forced interpretation. The author's untimely death left the

175

third volume unfinished. Other studies, therefore, should be consulted for discussions of twentieth-century literature, of which Alfred Kazin's recent *On Native Ground* seems to be the most thoughtful and sensitive.

For those who wish to understand the development of American government, the best single volume study is A. C. McLaughlin, *Constitutional History of the United States*. An interesting and important approach is given in A. P. Brigham, *Geographic Influence in American History,* and E. C. Semple, *American History and Its Geographic Influences.*

An able, and so far the only comprehensive, study of immigration to the United States is Carl Wittke, *We Who Built America.* For the older migration distinguished studies have been written by Marcus W. Hansen, *The Atlantic Migration, 1607-1860,* and *The Immigrant in American History.* The only study of the German contribution is A. B. Faust, *The German Element in the United States,* 2 volumes.

BIOGRAPHY:

The quickest and most satisfactory way of becoming acquainted with American issues and statesmen is through biography. This list is far from exhaustive and is intended only as an introduction. Additional titles can be found in the bibliographies to chapters in Morison and Commager.

The best study of the first American to achieve an international reputation is Carl Van Doren, *Benjamin Franklin.* No thoroughly satisfactory life of George Washington has yet appeared, but the most acceptable single-volume studies are P. L. Ford, *The True George Washington,* old but most commonly found in libraries, and Shelby Little, *George Washington.* Studies of Hamilton and Jefferson tend to be highly partisan, but David Loth, *Alexander Hamilton,* is judicious, and F. W. Hirst, *Life and Letters of Thomas Jefferson,* is a brilliant biography. One of the liveliest political biographies in our literature is Marquis James, *Andrew Jackson: Portrait of a President,* and a very readable study of one of his famous opponents is Claude M. Fuess, *Daniel Webster.* Fuess has also written our finest study of the most distinguished German immigrant to this country, *Carl Schurz.* Carl Sandburg, *Abraham Lincoln* is undoubtedly already classic, and gives virtually a history of Lincoln's period, but its 6 volumes are somewhat formidable at first. Good single-volume biographies are Lord Charnwood, *Abraham Lincoln,* and N. W. Stephenson, *Abraham Lincoln.*

Henry F. Pringle, *Theodore Roosevelt,* and William E. Dodd, *Woodrow Wilson,* are probably the best studies of these two presidents, to whose day we are still so close that impartial appraisal is difficult.

Special Studies:

It is difficult to choose from the hundreds of able and penetrating studies of special aspects of American history. The titles which follow have been selected with an eye to literary quality, the insights they provide into the factors which have produced the United States of today, and the possible interests of those consulting this book.

For the colonial and revolutionary period, S. E. Morison, *Builders of the Bay Colony,* and *The Maritime History of Massachusetts;* Carl Becker, *The Declaration of Independence,* and *The Eve of the Revolution;* J. F. Jameson, *The American Revolution Considered as a Social Movement.* For the great literary movement of the nineteenth century, Van Wyck Brooks, *The Flowering of New England,* and *New England: Indian Summer.* Frederick J. Turner called attention to the important role of the West in American development in *The Frontier in American History,* especially the first essay, "The Significance of the Frontier." Professor Turner's studies have had a profound influence on American historians, whether or not they accept his thesis. See also F. L. Paxson, *The History of the American Frontier.* For the development of the "old" West between the Appalachians and the Mississippi, F. J. Turner, *The Rise of the New West.* The growth of the West beyond the Mississippi is made vivid in a group of novels: Willa Cather, *O Pioneers,* Hamlin Garland, *A Son of the Middle Border,* Edna Ferber, *Cimarron,* Herbert Quick, *Vandemark's Folly* and *Hawkeye,* Owen Wister, *The Virginian.* For the history of sectionalism, almost as important an influence as the West, see Frederick J. Turner, *The Significance of the Sections in American History,* and Walter P. Webb, *Divided We Stand,* a survey of contemporary sectionalism. For the Civil War, C. R. Fish, *The American Civil War,* a provocative and penetrating study, and J. G. Randall, *The Civil War and Reconstruction,* scholarly and comprehensive with excellent bibliographies. For the rehabilitation of the South after the Civil War, Paul H. Buck, *The Road to Reunion.* The economic expansion of the post-Civil War period is judiciously presented in Cochran and Miller, *The Age of Enterprise.* Gustavus Meyers, *The History of Great American Fortunes,* is well known, highly readable, but propagandistic, and should be balanced by Allan Nevins' scholarly, impartial, and well-written *John D. Rocke-*

feller: The Heroic Age of American Enterprise. The reform movement of the early twentieth century is ably presented in John Chamberlain, *Farewell to Reform;* the best personal account is *The Autobiography of Lincoln Steffens,* one of the most active men in the movement. For twentieth-century United States, Dwight Dumond, *Roosevelt to Roosevelt,* offers the best general account. Walter Millis, *The Road to War,* is a trenchant but somewhat controversial account of the years 1914–1917. More conventional but less readable is Charles Seymour, *American Diplomacy during the World War,* and *American Neutrality.* The most judicious survey of American foreign policy since the first World War is D. F. Fleming, *The United States and World Organization, 1920–1933. R. S.* and Helen Lynd, *Middletown* and *Middletown in Transition,* are masterly case studies of life in a typical Mid-Western town, satirized in Sinclair Lewis, *Main Street.* Joseph Wood Krutch, *The Modern Temper,* offers an incisive study of the American frame of mind in the post-war years.

LIST OF BOOKS
FREQUENTLY QUOTED FROM
OR CONSULTED

I. SCHOLARLY GRAMMARS:

Curme, George O. *Syntax,* the third volume of the 3-volume Curme and Kurath, *Grammar of the English Language.* Published by D. C. Heath and Company.

Fries, Charles Carpenter. *American English Grammar.* The grammatical structure of present-day American English with especial reference to social differences or class dialects. Published by D. Appleton-Century Company.

Jespersen, Otto. *A Modern English Grammar on Historical Principles,* in 4 volumes. Published by Carl Winters Universitaets Buchhandlung.

The books listed above are indispensable to anyone who has a scholarly interest in English grammar.

II. PHONETICS OF BRITISH AND AMERICAN ENGLISH:

Ripman, Walter. *English Phonetics.* Published by J. M. Dent and Sons.

O'Neill, James M. *Foundations of Speech* by Professors Wise, McBurney, Mallory, Strother, and Temple, under the editorial direction of James M. O'Neill. Published by Prentice-Hall.

III. COLLEGE GRAMMARS AND HANDBOOKS:

Curme, George O. *College English Grammar.* Published by Johnson Publishing Company.

Hodges, John C. *Harbrace Handbook of English*. Published by Harcourt, Brace and Co.

Kierzek, John M. *The Macmillan Handbook of English*. Published by The Macmillan Company.

Aronstein, Philip. *Englische Schulstilistik*. Published by B. G. Teubner.

Deutschbein, Max. *Grammatik der Englischen Sprache*. Published by Quelle und Meyer.

IV. Modern British English and American Usage:

Fowler, H. W. *A Dictionary of Modern English Usage*. Published by the Oxford University Press. A useful book on usage, though occasionally contemptuous of current American and British usage.

Marckwardt, Albert H., and Walcott, Fred G. *Facts about Current English Usage*. Published by D. Appleton-Century Company. Contains the study by Sterling A. Leonard, *Current English Usage*.

Mencken, H. L. *The American Language. An Inquiry into the Development of English in the United States*. Published by Alfred A. Knopf. A provocative book on the differences between British and American English.

Index